3/84

Jim –

So why does a musical
wunderkind like you want to
read a book on an amusical
'jemand' like Lenin, anyway?
I hope you enjoy it — even
though the theatrics are of a
decidedly non-Schubertian
variety!

Elyse

ELYSE
TOPALIAN

V.I. LENIN

FRANKLIN WATTS
NEW YORK | LONDON | TORONTO | SYDNEY | 1983
AN IMPACT BIOGRAPHY

A GROLIER COMPANY

TO MY
PARENTS

Cover photograph courtesy of
United Press International

Photographs courtesy of
Sovfoto: pp. 9, 31;
Tass from Sovfoto: pp. 22, 112;
Soviet Life from Sovfoto: p. 42;
United Press International Photo: p. 45;
Culver Pictures: pp. 72, 89, 94, 107.

Library of Congress Cataloging in Publication Data

Topalian, Elyse.
V.I. Lenin.

(An Impact biography)
Bibliography: p.
Includes index.
Summary: Traces the life and assesses the influence
of the leader of the 1917 Bolshevik Revolution who
formulated the official Communist ideology and became
the first head of the Soviet state.
1. Lenin, Vladimir Il'ich, 1870–1924—Juvenile
literature. 2. Heads of state—Soviet Union—Biography
—Juvenile literature. 3. Revolutionists—Soviet Union
—Biography—Juvenile literature. [1. Lenin, Vladimir
Il'ich, 1870–1924. 2. Heads of state. 3.Revolutionists.
4. Communists. 5. Soviet Union—History] I. Title.
DK254.L455T66 1983 947.084′1′0924 [92] 82-21871
ISBN 0-531-04589-7

CONTENTS

V.I. LENIN

INTRODUCTION

A professor of Russian literature was recently planning to take his family on an extended trip to the Soviet Union. He told his thirteen-year-old son, Matty, to go to the local library in their small Connecticut town to find a book on Vladimir Ilich Lenin, since it is impossible to understand life in the Soviet Union today without first understanding its founding father. Matty went to the librarian and asked if there were any books available on Lenin. The librarian asked him, "John Lennon?"

Granted, John Lennon's influence on our lives has been profound. But all too often in the Western world, we underestimate the role that Vladimir Lenin played in shaping the character of the twentieth century. In his lifetime, Lenin oversaw the most far-reaching revolution of all time, a revolution that in 1917 radically altered the political and social structure of Russia and the balance of power throughout the world. Out of the large, cumbersome, backward Russia of the czars emerged a huge, modernized, Soviet dictatorship that is stronger now than ever before. From the original Communist regime that Lenin founded, a belief in Marxist thought has spread to presently encompass more than one-third of the people on earth. It is quite possible that this Lenin, a man of humble beginnings who never expected to live long enough to see his dream of revolution come true, had a greater impact on our time than just about any other single person who existed before him.

If the West tends to forget just how important Lenin was, though, the Communist countries carry their recognition of him to the opposite extreme. In the Soviet Union, Lenin is treated not simply as an important historical figure, but rather as a god. To the Soviets, his public image is one of seeming infallibility; he is presented as wise, strong, courageous, and kind. Lenin's likeness and words pervade every level of daily life—billboards, monuments, newspapers, broadcasts, even storybooks. Children are taught to follow his example of how to behave, how to dress, how to brush their teeth. In his name, adults are barraged with advice on how to become worthy citizens, hard workers, loyal Communists. Since the revolution, more than 350 million copies of works by Lenin have been published in the USSR alone. Lenin is omnipresent. He is the ultimate mentor and guide for all Soviets, the final authority on every aspect of life and understanding.

Any Westerner who visits the Soviet Union is bound to be shocked by the pervasiveness of Lenin's influence and by the utter extravagance of his nation's adulation for him. Part of the shock stems from lack of Western corollaries—we have no cult heroes here who are treated with anything approaching such regard. Apart from the legends about chopping down the cherry tree and throwing a silver dollar across the Potomac, how much does the average American know about George Washington? What percentage of the American population can quote past the first line of the Gettysburg Address or remember how many brothers and sisters Lincoln had? To witness firsthand how the Soviets elevate Lenin inevitably inspires some guilt in Americans about the relative lack of attention to our own revolutionary past. But the extremes to which the worship of Lenin is carried also raise some serious questions about who Lenin *really* was—what he thought, what he did, what he wanted to do. In the Soviet Union today, the man and the myth are often difficult to distinguish.

Lenin's likeness appears before the Russians so many times and in so many ways and shapes, that he becomes easy to ignore. In a park in Kiev a floral arrangement is fashioned, quite successfully, to resemble Lenin's face. In classrooms, concert halls, movie theaters, and hotels his likeness stares down on the population. At the Bay of Finland, where Lenin once went into hiding before the revolution, visitors are shown a tree stump on which he had supposedly sat to write an essay, a haystack (more like an igloo) in which he had supposedly camouflaged himself, and a small cottage in which he had stayed (now totally encased by a huge glass box).

In Moscow, the adulation reaches its absurd height. There, in Red Square, people wait in a long, winding line to see Lenin's tomb. The line crawls past an eternal flame honoring the millions of Russians who died during World War II, across the vast cobblestone expanse of the square, toward a low, inconspicuous building just outside the wall of the Kremlin. The building is labeled, simply, "LENIN." Soldiers with rifles are stationed at the doorway, their eyes constantly roving about to make sure that everyone follows instructions. Inside, at last, one meets Lenin himself. In the recessed center of the room, in a brightly lit coffin of glass, lies the embalmed Vladimir Ilich Lenin. He has been dead for more than half a century, but time has not aged him. He lies calmly, hands over chest, utterly oblivious to his constant companions, the armed sentries and the steady stream of gawkers passing a few yards away.

In his resting place, Lenin looks waxen and small. The imperfect glass of the coffin ripples, creating a hazy, dreamlike image that forces a visitor to wonder what one really sees in that room. Is it Lenin or just another likeness of him? Many Russians and tourists are convinced that the tomb houses nothing more than a well-crafted wax doll. Whatever the case, the Soviet government will not allow Lenin to die. And in forcing him to live forever, they have taken away his humanity.

Who was Lenin, really—not the god, but the man? Where did he come from, what did he believe in? How did he manage to catch the fancy of an entire nation at a crucial point in history and then convince that nation to mold itself according to his personal vision? Did he love? Did he hate? Did he ever fail? And finally, why have his people chosen to immortalize him so relentlessly? How does Lenin's memory—whether that memory is based on facts or on legends—serve the needs and interests of the Soviet Union today?

Clearly Lenin was never simply just a hero *or* a villain. He had an enigmatic personality that shines through the Soviet whitewash. On the Beatles' *White Album* John Lennon sang, "You say you want a revolution / Well you know / we all want to change the world." Vladimir Ilich Lenin dreamt of a revolution that would bring a better life and society. What made him extraordinary was that he wanted to change the world, and, against all odds, he did. This is the story of *how* he did.

LIFE ALONG THE VOLGA

1

For many Russians, the Volga River symbolizes the very heart and blood of the nation. The long, slow, monotonous river rises in the north between Moscow and Leningrad, then winds its way southeast past the cities of Kazan, Simbirsk, Saratov, and Astrakhan to empty into the Caspian Sea. Along its path, revolutionary uprisings by peasants and Cossacks in the seventeenth and eighteenth centuries took place, creating a tradition and an intensity that still linger on. The Volga has always been considered the dividing line between Europe and Asia, since the two shores—endless plains of Asiatic steppes on one side versus gently rolling hills and bluffs on the other—are as different culturally as they are geographically.

Lenin spent his first twenty-three years in towns along the Volga. At that time, in the second half of the nineteenth century, life was as slow-paced and monotonous as the river. The songs, chants, and legends of the Volga boatmen were still very much alive, and peasants continued to haul barges along by ropes and sheer human strength. The more progressive, showy steamboats were just starting to make their appearance in significant numbers, bringing in new kinds of trade to the quiet river communities. Like people living on the great American Mississippi River in the same period, the Volga townspeople had their own simple culture and lifestyle, which may have seemed backward or uncivilized in comparison with much of the rest of the world, but which was firmly linked to the river for both physical and spiritual sustenance. The young Lenin spent much of his time hiking or rowing along the river with his older brother, sometimes exploring waterways or riding on steamboats for a week at a time. And, although in later life he aspired to a much more modernized sort of existence for Russia and rarely ventured out of the large cities of Europe and Russia himself, Lenin would often rhapsodize about the beautiful simplicity and the characteristic culture of life along the Volga.

Lenin, whose name was originally Ulyanov, was born in the backwater town of Simbirsk in 1870. Simbirsk, a conservative provincial capital on the European shore of the Volga, was a poor, sleepy town of about thirty thousand that was not significant enough as a river port to warrant a railway connection to the rest of the countryside. Rutted dirt roads linked the modest wooden buildings that were scattered among the hills, and from the highest promontory in town stared down a drab complex of stone houses that included a school, library, prison, cathedral, and governor's mansion. Lush apple and cherry orchards filled the hills with blossoms and fragrance in the spring, and after the river's swelling caused by melting winter snows had gone down, a thick mat of green grass covered its banks.

The Ulyanovs lived on the second floor of a plain, square-framed house, situated on a bluff at the edge of town. Ilya Nikolayevich Ulyanov, Lenin's father, was a short, balding man with a bushy, reddish beard and moustache who, by all accounts, was earnestly devoted to his work, his family, and his Russian Orthodox faith. The son of a poor tailor from Astrakhan, he had worked his way through school and the university by tutoring and teaching privately, then had landed a job as senior teacher of physics and mathematics at a prestigious institute in Penza. After he married Maria Alexandrovna Blank in 1863, he was promoted to director of public schools for a district that ran three hundred miles from north to south along the Volga. This position won him the honor of a title of hereditary nobility under the czar's system of ranking, but it also meant that he had to travel a lot, by train and by horseback. He was often away from his family for several weeks at a time.

In his seventeen years as an educational director, Ilya Nikolayevich was responsible for the construction of around 450 new schools in his district, causing the student population to double. Much of his spare time was spent tutoring remedial and underprivileged students without charge. Yet, although he was a liberalizing force by his efforts to provide educational opportunities to a backward area, Ilya Nikolayevich was indisputably a loyal subject of the czar and a firm believer in the church, in no conscious way laying a foundation for his son's future revolutionary beliefs.

Lenin's mother, Maria Alexandrovna Ulyanov, came from quite a different background than her husband. She was the daughter of a doctor who practiced mainly in St. Petersburg and who owned a country estate in Kazan. Although she never had any formal schooling, she could speak four languages fluently and was well versed in history, music, and literature. She kept a tidy, orderly household, and had a personality that was always even-tempered, kind, and strong. Since Simbirsk was so removed from the culture and progress of the city environment in which she had been raised, and because her husband was away from home so much of the time, Maria Alexandrovna must have often felt isolated and alone. She devoted herself entirely to the education and comfort of her family, and, although she did not live long enough to see the revolution of 1917, she stood by all her children through the personal hardships and political struggles in the pre-revolutionary years. Lenin held a very special place in his heart for her.

The Ulyanovs had six children, of which Vladimir, the future Lenin, was the third. Anna, born in 1864, was the oldest; she would later recall their childhood as "cloudless and happy." Alexander, often called Sasha, arrived two years later, and, although he was four years older and never very close to Vladimir, he exerted by far the greatest influence of all the siblings on the revolutionary leader-to-be. In the early years, Vladimir looked to Alexander as a role model, even when making the smallest decisions; when asked if he wanted to go outside to play or take milk in his hot cereal, he would inevitably answer, "The same as Sasha." Vladimir, born in 1870, was named after the saint who converted Russia to Eastern Orthodox Christianity in the tenth century. After him came Olga in 1871, Dmitri in 1874, and Maria in 1878.

Vladimir was always boisterous and energetic as a child, and his siblings remembered him as one who was always more likely to break his toys than to play with them. He was nicknamed "Kubyshkin" or "the bellied jug" because he was so short and stocky. When he was learning to walk, he had a hard time balancing his bulky frame, so time after time he would fall down on his nose and then let out piercing screams. As the years went by, Vladimir grew to look more and more like his father, with slanting gray eyes and high cheekbones that betrayed an almost Mongolian cast, and reddish hair that would start to recede even before he had reached twenty years of age. But as a child, he was simply a compact, intense bundle of energy.

Vladimir was a ringleader of sorts, always inventing games, making jokes, and playing pranks. He liked to make noise and never minded getting into trouble for it. At home he would tease his younger sister Olga endlessly, and as a result was often sent to sit quietly in a black chair in the study for

This photograph of the Ulyanov family was taken in 1879 when Vladimir (seated at right) was nine years old.

penance. But the punishments never seemed to bother him; more than once he simply went to sleep in the "dreaded" chair.

The younger children, especially, looked to Vladimir for creative entertainment. One of their favorite games would take place when both parents were out of the house. Vladimir would pull all the curtains closed and blow out all the lamps, then sit Dmitri and Olga down on the floor of one room and retreat into another. Suddenly, he would return as the *brykaska*, or "bucking bronco" monster. The mood of the *brykaska* was unpredictable; the children might have to run from him if he was angry or dance around with him if he was jolly. The game kept them all busy and excited for hours on end.

With his older brother, Alexander, Vladimir played games that were more sophisticated and often oriented to the outdoors. The two brothers were markedly different in personality and physical appearance. Alexander was a dreamer, a quiet and introspective boy with pale white skin and thick, frizzy hair who stood tall and thin. No matter what his mood, Vladimir, with his Mongolian features and round head, never ceased to be noisy, self-confident, and aggressive. But Vladimir and Alexander made good companions, fishing and swimming together in the summer, skating and skiing in the winter, and playing chess all year round in the hope of one day being able to beat their father.

Duplicity was a trait foreign to Alexander. Once, when asked by a teacher to name the worst possible vices, he replied, "lying and cowardice," and, by all accounts, he was always truthful and honorable in his words and actions. Vladimir placed his priorities somewhat differently. Although he was certainly not habitually a dishonest child, he was caught from time to time in a lie. Once, for example, he denied breaking a vase of his mother's, and then three months later tearfully admitted the misdeed. Later in life, as a revolutionary, Vladimir told his followers that it was all right to lie in certain instances to achieve one's ends.

Vladimir's trickiness, as in military play, often baffled his siblings. His favorite pastime was playing soldier, and he would tirelessly drill the other children in the yard in back of their house. Indoors, they would command armies of soldiers and generals cut from heavy paper and colored in with crayons. Vladimir's army would inevitably be American; he would pretend to be Abraham Lincoln, giving orders to his generals, Grant and Sherman. Alexander played Garibaldi at the head of the Italian troops, while Anna and Olga led the Spanish forces. Once, in a skirmish with Dmitri's army, Vladimir executed a crafty maneuver. When the battle began and the commanders launched their dried peas across the dining room table at the opposing forces, Dmitri's soldiers fell down when hit whereas Vladimir's kept popping back up. It turned out that Vladimir had fastened his paper dolls to the table with light nails so that they could not go down in battle.

The family drew closest together in the winter, when the Volga would freeze over, almost completely cutting Simbirsk off from contact with the rest of the world. Ilya Nikolayevich and Maria Alexandrovna would make the Christmas season a very festive time, putting their children to work on decorations and presents as soon as the snows started to fall in November. The family would sing hymns together with Maria Alexandrovna at the piano, and on Christmas Eve the candles on the tree would be lit, gifts would be presented, and the children would recite verses by heart. One memorable Christmas Eve, Alexander chose to recite some of his father's favorite lines from Ryleyev's "A Life for the Czar." A line that he spoke most passionately that day would ironically become the epitaph on his gravestone when he died tragically a few years later: "He who is Russian in his heart is brave and bold and happy to die in the right cause."

During the rest of the year, most family activities centered around learning. The Ulyanovs kept a wide range of books shelved around the house, from Russian classics by Lermontov, Pushkin, and Gogol, to adventure stories from abroad by Jules Verne, Sir Walter Scott, James Fenimore Cooper, and Daniel Defoe. Maria Alexandrovna taught each of her children to read as soon as they were able; Vladimir and Olga learned at the same time, when he was five and she was four. Alexander loved to read and would always have his head in a book. Vladimir read a lot, too, but he was more selective; *Ivanhoe* was his personal favorite.

Because his mother undertook the early formal education of all her children by herself (and later with the help of some private tutors that the family could eventually afford), Vladimir did not enter the local public school system until he was nine years old. As soon as he did, it became clear that his behavior in class was far more controlled and obedient that otherwise. At home, he had always been boisterous and bossy, with a quick temper, but in school, he was a model of good conduct. Like his siblings, Vladimir rose immediately to the top of his class and stayed there until he graduated at the age of seventeen. He worked so quickly and systematically, and had such a good memory, that whenever his father would test him on his homework, he would invariably know all the right answers.

The meticulousness with which Vladimir prepared his essays for school showed off the superb organizational skills that would dominate his revolutionary work later in life. According to his brother Dmitri, as soon as an essay was assigned, Vladimir would draw up an outline that included an introduction and a conclusion. Then he would fold a fresh piece of paper down the middle and on the left side of it would compose a roughdraft of the essay. The right side was eventually filled up with notes and scribbles concerning the corrections, modifications and expansions that occurred to him as he brooded over the draft. Finally, just before his deadline, he would combine all the materials to arrive at a final version of the essay.

Fyodor Kerensky, the director of the school—and, ironically, the father of the political leader, Alexander Kerensky, whose government the mature Lenin would overthrow—took a special interest in Vladimir, and later played an important role in his education. The boy got a five (the Russian equivalent of an A) in every subject in high school except logic. The humanities—Russian literature, Greek, and Latin— were his strong favorites, and he had shown some talent for music when he had studied piano as a child. But these were interests that he increasingly veered away from in adulthood. He came to believe that such subjects were "dangerous addictions" that could only divert revolutionaries from pure political thoughts and actions.

Ilya Nikolayevich faced some personal disappointments during the years that his eldest children were in high school. First, in 1881 Czar Alexander II was assassinated. This was a great blow to Ilya Nikolayevich who, upon hearing the news, went home to don his uniform and then went to pray at the cathedral. Not only did Ilya Nikolayevich detest violence, but he also held high hopes for what he felt was the liberalizing force of the czar's expansive view toward education.

Another dissappointment befell Ilya Nikolayevich when Alexander informed his father that he no longer believed in God. Ilya Nikolayevich had been raised in the Russian Orthodox faith and had remained devout throughout his lifetime, but Maria Alexandrovna had never felt comfortable with the rituals of the church. Although the Ulyanovs had observed religious holidays at home with their children, Ilya Nikolayevich had often gone to worship alone. Alexander's proclamation of atheism undoubtedly hurt his father, but Ilya Nikolayevich accepted his son's decision and never brought up the subject again.

A few years later, when he was sixteen, Vladimir reached the same philosophical crossroad as his brother. Later in life, he would describe the turning point to his friend Krzhizhanovsky by saying that as soon as he realized there was no God, he removed the cross from around his neck, spat on it, and discarded it. The account may or may not be true, but it certainly describes a very important characteristic of Lenin the revolutionary: once he had made up his mind about something, he acted on his decision and never looked back. As with Alexander's previous announcement, Vladimir's rejection of God was quietly accepted by Ilya Nikolayevich.

And then in 1886 the Ulyanov family suffered the first of two tragedies that would bring its relatively happy era to a close. That January, Ilya Nikolayevich died suddenly of a cerebral hemmorhage. All of the children were shaken by their father's death, but Alexander, who now considered himself the head of the household, took the news especially hard. Anna and Alexander were away from home, studying at the university in St. Petersburg, and for days Alexander just walked back and forth in his room, neglecting everything. One of his friends reported that he was even contemplating suicide. But his mother would not allow either him or his sister Anna to return to Simbirsk. Such was the Ulyanov tradition of always putting education and sense of duty first, and Alexander lived up to his parents' ideal of devotion to duties by winning a gold medal that season for excellence in his zoological studies.

Alexander had been absorbed in the sciences for a long time already. While still in high school, he had converted one of the rooms in the Ulyanov house into a "laboratory," where he conducted his chemical and biological experiments and from which he scarcely budged. Alexander found the intellectual atmosphere of the university much more stimulating than that of his secondary school, which he had considered too rigid. During his first three years at the university, he buried himself in biological research, barely spending any time with other students and scorning all organized student activities such as clubs, which he dismissed by saying, "One talks a lot there, and learns nothing."

Alexander spent the summer after his father died with the rest of the Ulyanovs at the country estate of his mother's family in Kokushkino. Other than being extra mindful that his bereaved mother was always treated with respect and compassion, he was as obsessed with science as ever. About to begin his fourth year at the university, Alexander was preoccupied with his dissertation topic, a study of the Annelida phylum of earthworms. Vladimir, who shared a room with his brother at the estate, watched Alexander get up early every morning to take advantage of the best light for his microscope. He later remembered that a strange thought crossed his mind: "My brother will never become a revolutionary. A revolutionary cannot spend so much time on annelids."

But Vladimir was wrong. Even before the summer at Kokushkino with his family, Alexander had begun to change his mind about the value of student organizations and had participated in a group demonstration at Volkov Cemetery in St. Petersburg in honor of the officials who had been responsible for emancipating the serfs. He had also taken a leadership role in the formation of a federation of students from a wide cross section of provinces. Books by radical, revolutionary writers like Chernyshevsky and Pisarev began to win him over.

Alexander never let these activities interfere with his studies, and he never mentioned them to his family. And so, in March 1887, when the news reached Simbirsk that he had been arrested in St. Petersburg for taking part in a revolutionary group that had plotted to assassinate Czar Alexander III, it came as quite a shock.

Maria Alexandrovna decided to go to St. Petersburg at once to see her son. It would be a difficult journey since the Volga was still frozen over and the only access to the railroad in Sizran was by horseback. News had spread quickly through Simbirsk about the sort of political trouble that Alexander was in. Although the Ulyanovs had always been one of the most highly respected families in town, when Maria Alexandrovna approached friends and associates to see if anyone could possibly accompany her on her journey, she found herself snubbed by everyone. She went alone to ask Alexander to plead for a pardon so that he would not be executed for high treason.

Vladimir was left to watch over the rest of the family. He himself had never been very interested in politics. His brother's secret side surprised and puzzled him, and the seriousness of Alexander's predicament upset him greatly. But he was about to finish his final year of high school in Simbirsk. In typical Ulyanov fashion, he devoted himself to preparing for his upcoming exams and graduation as best he could.

A LIFE FOR THE CZAR

2

The charge against Alexander Ulyanov, bizarre as it may
have seemed to his family, was not a fabrication. He had
indeed plotted to kill the czar. But whereas the violent nature
of Alexander's newfound political involvement was a brutal
shock to those who knew him as a quiet, idealistic and impassioned youth, his beliefs and actions were not at all out of
step with the times. Russia in 1887 was painfully backward
with respect to the rest of the world, and life was difficult for
the majority of its people, the peasant masses. Alexander
was merely one of the newcomers to the ranks of a long line
of radicals who felt compelled to bring about, by whatever
means necessary, such revolutionary changes as would raise
the quality of existence in Russia.

The museum in the Kremlin today holds the remnants of
the awesome wealth that the czars and the nobility enjoyed
over several centuries: crowns, scepters, Bibles, and earrings
studded with priceless jewels so large as to seem fake; car-
riages made of solid gold; tapestries of the finest silk with
pearls and rubies sometimes woven into them. Czar Alexander III, with his palaces and yachts and Cossack guards, was

the absolute ruler of Russia in the 1880s. Yet the world that he and his small circle inhabited was more accurately a reflection of the culture and temperament of Western Europe than of the mass suffering in his own floundering empire.

Most people in the vast expanse of Russia would never lay eyes on the czar but would only hear vague stories about him and his way of life. Ninety-five percent of the population was illiterate. Serfs, or peasants, had been freed from bondage to the landowners only a generation before, but their depressed life-style remained basically the same. In the 1880s the peasants or "black people," as they were called, still eked out meager livings by breaking their backs pulling boats down the river, sledges across roads, and ploughs across fields. They were so prone to disease and starvation that the average life span barely exceeded thirty years.

Across the pitiful squalor of the land swept the unstoppable current of the new industrial age, which had originated in Western Europe several decades before. With the coming of the railroad and the steam engine, Russia took heart. Peasants swarmed to the cities looking for work in the oil fields and the textile mills and the new steel industries. But they were not long in finding out that any salvation promised by the new age was purely illusory.

True, Russia doubled its industrial production and the number of workers in industry during the short period from 1865 to 1890. But the accompanying exploitation of the industrial workers brought harder times than were ever seen under the feudal system of serfdom.

Workers were housed in contaminated wooden barracks that had no heat and were forced to take work shifts that were commonly as long as fifteen hours or more without rest. The pay was a mere pittance—around thirty or forty kopecks a day (around twenty-five cents then). Despite widespread brutality, even murder, which the Cossack guards directed against those who dared to work slowly or to complain about their conditions, strikes among textile, steel, and iron mill workers became more and more common (there were 326 reported strikes in the 1870s, compared with 446 in the five-year period from 1880 to 1885). But the strikes had a minimal effect. Returning to the farms was useless, since the new *kulak* system gave rise to a class of greedy, wealthy landlords who paid their help even lower wages than the factory owners did. The workers were trapped.

Teachers in rural areas were in a similarly tragic plight. By 1902 as many as eleven thousand of them were near starvation. They earned an average of one-and-a-half to two rubles (around one dollar) a week and were often housed right in their own tiny schoolrooms, in unheated sheds, or in barns alongside the peasants' livestock.

In a way, the fact that this situation percolated for so long without erupting into a mass revolt was surprising. Group action was, in retrospect, the only hope that the lower classes had of improving their living and working arrangements. But at the time, the czar and his Cossack forces managed to keep the workers in line with their strict measures and their harsh reprisals for disobedience or laziness.

Nevertheless, a strong undercurrent of dissent was developing, not among the workers themselves, but among a class of people called the *intelligentsia*. The intelligentsia was held together not by a common social background, but rather by a shared set of liberal, idealistic, humanitarian beliefs, and a strong faith in the power of the idea and the word to transform society for the better. It had its roots in the early nineteenth century, when Russian troops returned home from the Napoleonic wars filled with the spirit and ideas of the recent French Revolution. Many of the officers met secretly to plot some form of political protest against the czar's regime. On December 26, 1825, after the death of Czar Alexander I, they marched into the coronation ceremony in St. Petersburg to demand that Constantine, and not his brother the Grand Duke Nicholas, become the new czar. But the revolt was quickly fired upon and disbanded by loyal government forces, and those "Decembrists" (as they became known) who were caught faced execution, long sentences of hard labor, or Siberian exile.

Over the next few decades, a pattern of underground

conspiracy and government retribution developed. The secret groups that would meet to discuss political, social, and literary problems were composed mainly of students, professors, and even some members of the nobility. They looked consistently to the French radicals and German idealists for their inspiration, but were at a loss as to how to organize a revolution in their own country. In London, from 1857 to 1861, Alexander Herzen successfully published an oppositional newspaper called *The Bell* and had it smuggled into Russia. But censorship at home was strict, and arrests of such writers as Turgenev and Dostoyevsky were common because they either displeased the censors or participated in underground literary groups.

In the 1860s, when hopes for liberalization under the new czar, Alexander II, did not materialize and the emancipated serfs grew increasingly bitter and oppressed, the philosophies of the liberal intellectuals became more out-and-out revolutionary. Mikhail Bakunin, a member of the nobility and a former artillery officer, preached the destruction of the existing order so that a new one could be established, based on atheism, free education for all, equality of the sexes, and control of land not by private owners but by agricultural communes and labor associations. Sergei Nechayev, his follower, headed a secret society of a few hundred people who planned to bring about mass insurrection through terrorist activities, which were supposedly justifiable because Nechayev felt that any means of bringing about revolution was moral. After an act of indiscriminate violence revealed Nechayev's plottings and his group was broken apart by arrests, a more reasonable and visionary man named Peter Lavrov gained prominence in revolutionary circles. Lavrov believed, like the others, in the necessity of revolution but felt that the end did not justify the means. Terrorist insurrection, if successful, would only transfer the vast power of the czarist regime to a small revolutionary elite. The masses were not ready for revolution, so he advocated a period of gradual education for them, in which they would be apprised of their needs and goals.

But the peasants, however bleak their existence, did not respond well enough to the propagandistic efforts of these revolutionaries who were trying to instigate uprisings and strikes. So, in 1879, when all other means had seemingly failed, a group called "Land and Freedom" that had drawn its inspiration from Bakunin as well as Lavrov voted to rename itself *Narodnaya Volya* ("The People's Will") and turned to open terrorism.

The czar was their prime target. For almost two years, members of the People's Will stalked him, but none of their assassination attempts were successful. Many times they tried to blow up his train, but for one reason or another, their intricate schemes always failed. When a bomb finally exploded in the dining room of one of the czar's palaces, he escaped injury because he had happened to leave the room just a few moments before.

Ironically, the attempt that finally succeeded in killing Alexander II occurred on the very same day that he signed into law a liberalizing measure providing for elected government officials that might have eventually paved the way for a constitution in Russia. On March 1, 1881, however, the terrorists threw a bomb at the czar's carriage as it traveled through the streets of St. Petersburg. Two people, not including Alexander II, lay wounded, and when the czar got out of his carriage to see if they were all right, a second bomb killed him and the terrorist who held it.

This was the murder that so upset Lenin's father, Ilya Nikolayevich Ulyanov, in faraway Simbirsk. In fact, Russian society at large was shocked and revulsed. Rumors even spread through the lower classes that evil landlords had arranged to kill the czar because he had been sympathetic toward the peasants. When the surviving People's Will members were captured and brought to trial, their eloquent denunciations of the autocracy reaped only a sparse show of public sympathy. The terrorists had reached their immediate goal of destroying the czar but had failed in the long term. After the executions, only a few flickering embers remained of the People's Will movement.

In the years after 1881, several isolated attempts to revive the organization were made. Despite ever harsh and swift reprisals by the government, terrorists managed to assassinate a few key officials, including an infamous Odessa policeman named Strelnikov, and Sudeikin, head of the czar's secret police. Demonstrations at the universities increased in number. It was in this atmosphere of seething political unrest that Alexander Ulyanov took part in an attempt to kill the new czar, Alexander III.

Alexander had become convinced of the need for violent action against the czarist regime when a peaceful demonstration in which he had participated at the Volkov Cemetery in St. Petersburg had been brutally disbanded by the police. He joined a rather bumbling and disorganized student group that called itself the "Terrorist Faction of the People's Will." In actual fact, none of the members had any terrorist experience. Yet together they hatched a plan to assassinate the czar, and on the night before their attempt, they set about drawing up a manifesto for themselves.

Alexander was their secretary. He recorded a hodgepodge of group demands, all based on past People's Will platforms, including free popular elections, full and equal rights for all citizens, nationalization of land and industry, free education, and amnesty for all political prisoners. He began the essay, "The spirit of the Russian land lives and the truth is not extinguished in the hearts of her sons."

On March 1, 1887, exactly six years after People's Will terrorists had successfully murdered the former czar, Alexander's group lay in wait for Alexander III's carriage along the Nevsky Prospect, St. Petersburg's widest boulevard. The carriage never arrived, and when the revolutionaries retired to a local tavern, they were arrested by the police, who had been shadowing a member of their group for days. Later, it was determined that even if the makeshift bombs had been thrown, defective fuses would have prevented them from exploding. These pitiful circumstances were made worse by the discovery of an address book in code that Alexander was carrying. Once the code was cracked, a network of revolu-

tionaries throughout Russia was uncovered, resulting in scores of more arrests. Fifteen members of Alexander's immediate group were scheduled for trial.

Seven days after he was thrown in jail, Maria Alexandrovna arrived in St. Petersburg to try to help Alexander. For weeks, she was denied entrance to see him, until finally she wrote a personal plea to the czar. Her letter had the desired effect; the czar scribbled in one margin, "Let her see him so that she may witness for herself what kind of person her son has become." Alexander asked forgiveness of his mother for making her suffer, but would not follow her entreaties for him to petition for a pardon. Instead, at the trial, he not only presented his own defense but also took the blame for many of his co-conspirators' actions so as to lighten their sentences. The brilliance of Alexander's concluding speech dazzled his mother, who had never imagined that her quiet son had become so articulate. He drove home the point that, given the society's oppressed condition and despite its disapproval of violence, the only available road to constructive social action was terrorism. He was not afraid to die, he said, because he would be dying for the common good.

Not surprisingly, he was indeed sentenced by the court to die. On May 8, 1887, Alexander Ulyanov and four of his fellow terrorists were executed by hanging at an old stone fortress outside St. Petersburg called Shlisselburg. From two of the young men, a final cry rang out loud and clear: "Long live the People's Will!"

Alexander Ulyanov

THE BIRTH OF A NEW REVOLU-TIONARY

3

Back in Simbirsk, Vladimir reproached himself for having never really understood his brother. Over the next few years, he would become obsessed with getting to know what his dead brother had been like by questioning as many of Alexander's fellow students and revolutionaries as possible. Vladimir wanted to know about all the sides of Alexander's personality that he had overlooked, about Alexander's work and his philosophy of science, about the awakening and nature of Alexander's political beliefs. Supposedly, when Vladimir received the telegram bearing the news of his brother's execution, he cried out, "Well, then we shall not take that road. We shall take a different road." This comment may be pure myth. But whether it is or not, the death of Alexander did more than signal the politicization of Vladimir; it marked the birth of a new revolutionary.

For the time being, though, Vladimir had to concentrate on studying for his final exams, and this he did with what most people around him perceived as cold-blooded self-control. On the surface, Vladimir betrayed signs of grief only once. One May evening in 1887, when Dmitri Andreyev, a classmate, was walking along the Volga to take a break from his studies, he saw a hunched figure sitting under a distant gazebo. It was Vladimir, and he was so despondent that the two of them just stared silently at the water for a while. When Andreyev finally ventured to ask what was wrong, Vladimir told him that his brother had been executed in St. Petersburg. They walked slowly back into Simbirsk together, and Andreyev said that as they approached the town, Vladimir visibly regained control of himself. When they parted, Vladimir shook Andreyev's hands and stared into his eyes with an intensity that the friend would never forget.

With the exception of that evening, though, Vladimir never let down his guard, especially after the weight of his recent family tragedies was increased by the social stigma of being related to a terrorist revolutionary. He took his final oral and written examinations calmly and impassively, and was rated outstanding in all subjects. As the highest-ranking graduate, Vladimir, like his brother Alexander before him, received the school's gold medal.

The government might well have barred Vadimir from receiving a university education because of his brother's actions if Fyodor Kerensky, who remained a faithful and influential family friend, had not interceded. As the director of Vladimir's school and one of its teachers, Kerensky wrote such a strong letter of recommendation that Vladimir was admitted to Kazan University. That Vladimir should go to Kazan, in particular, was also Kerensky's idea. He thought it best that his student not go to school in any of the major cities of Russia, where the campuses were in such political turmoil. He suggested that Maria Alexandrovna accompany her son to his new environment so that she could watch over him and make sure that he stayed out of trouble. And so, shortly after Vladimir's graduation from high school, the Ulyanov family packed up and left Simbirsk to start a new life in Kazan.

Vladimir's father had attended Kazan University many years before, but in the fall of 1887, the mood on campus was dramatically different from when Ilya Nikolayevich had been there. The repercussions of the execution of Alexander and his friends had not been limited to St. Petersburg circles. Students in universities all over the country had reacted to the news with a wave of protests. And although the demonstrations diminished during the summer, when Vladimir moved to Kazan in the fall the student protests had started up again in a new surge.

The demonstrations of 1887 were only an extension of the tensions that had been building for many years, the same tensions that had given rise in the first place to groups like the People's Will. The government tried to foil all possibilities for organized dissent by using its power to regiment life at the universities as much as possible. To some degree, it had been successful. Dress code rules were now strictly enforced, so students had to wear uniforms instead of the shabby sort of attire that had become a symbol of protest. Each student had to pledge, on entering the university, that he or she would not join any organizations that were not specifically approved by the government. And an official called the student inspector, who served as a sort of spy for the police, had been instated in each institution. But these surface changes did not snuff out the dissent; in the long run, they only provided more fuel for student hostility toward the government's repressive regime. In the fall of 1887, the dam that the authorities had built started to burst.

As Vladimir was beginning his first-year studies in pursuit of a career in law (against the advice of Kerensky, who recommended a professorial job in the humanities instead), a student in Moscow slapped a student inspector during a concert. The harshness of the punishment—three years of military service in a regiment made up of criminals—sparked a series of protests and demonstrations, one of which was broken up by soldiers. The Kazan students then took up the cry. On December 16, a large group gathered in the university's auditorium to object to the happenings in Moscow and to demand changes in the government's restrictions on the universities. The crowd was boisterous but nonviolent until the student inspector appeared, demanding that they disperse. A few people cried out, "Get him!" and he was beaten up and ejected from the room. A full-scale riot ensued.

Vladimir was present at this disturbance. Because of his brother's notoriety he was watched closely by university authorities, and his reddish hair and clenched fists now made him especially conspicuous in the first row of the auditorium, even though he remained silent throughout the proceedings. When the crowd settled down, the students were marched out in single file and forced to show identification at the door. The officials needed to make an example of some of the demonstrators to the other students, and an Ulyanov provided a likely scapegoat. That evening Vladimir was arrested in his home. More than one hundred other students, comprising more than one-eighth of the entire student body, were arrested as well. Forty-five of them were expelled on the spot, and the rest were asked to resign from the university. All student activities and lectures were brought to a halt for two months.

Vladimir was expelled not only from the university, but also from the town of Kazan. His mother decided to move the family again, this time to Kokushkino, her family's estate, which—like Simbirsk and Kazan—was situated along the Volga River. Vladimir was given official permission to live at Kokushkino under police surveillance. As he was being escorted from Kazan, his police guard supposedly asked, "Why do you rebel, young man? You must realize that you are up against a wall." Vladimir was said to have replied: "A wall, yes, but it is rotten. One kick and it will crumble."

The quote reveals some of the important changes in Vladimir's personality that had taken place since his brother's death. No longer was Vladimir the carefree, lively youth of Simbirsk with no stake or particular interest in politics. He was, instead, an intense, introspective, and reticent young man who was starting to evolve a vision of revolutionary struggle and change. In Kazan he had been part of an underground circle led by Lazar Bogoraz, whose express aim was to rekindle the People's Will movement and to kill the czar. In retrospect, it seems almost as if he was trying to take up the cause exactly where his brother Alexander had left off.

In contrast to his political involvement in Kazan, Vladimir's life in Kokushkino started out to be dreadfully boring. He whiled away the time playing chess with his brother Dmitri and his sister Anna's fiancé, Elisarov. Only a few neighbors were bold enough to visit the big old house that the family occupied. Vladimir became a heavy smoker and browsed through the library of rather dated books that a deceased uncle had set up.

Then, suddenly, Vladimir started a new regimen. He stopped smoking all at once, walked and swam a lot, and immersed himself in the boxes of books that he borrowed by mail from the Kazan library. His utter self-discipline was astounding, and his methodical approach to everything was an attitude that he would retain for the rest of his life.

During this time, Vladimir read everything he could get his hands on, from poetry and literature to works on philosophy and economics. The book that affected Vladimir by far the most deeply, though, was a novel by Chernyshevsky called *What Is to Be Done?* The literary quality of the book was abysmal, yet it had become one of the mainstays of revolutionary thought in Russia. Vladimir had tried to read it when he was fourteen, but it had seemed superficial and its meaning had eluded him. Knowing that it had been one of his brother Alexander's favorite books, however, Vladimir tackled it again at Kokushkino and ended up reading it five times in sequence. "I pored over the book," he later remembered, "not several days but several weeks. Only then did I understand its full depth. It is a work that gives one a charge for a whole life."

What Is to Be Done? is an idealistic novel whose several themes captured the essence of late-nineteenth century revolutionary beliefs: that every human relationship should be based on an acceptance of the equality of all people, that communal living is one of the most important ways to do away with the imbalances in society, and that each person must be dedicated in mind, body, and spirit toward realizing his or her principles and aims. From the book, Vladimir assimilated two beliefs that would never leave him: first, the belief that the individual is the potential holder of great power, power that, when exercised, can influence events or even alter the course of history; and second, that total dedication to one's ideals means that any path toward achieving one's ends is valid and justifiable. Although this second conviction was one of the ground rules of terrorism, Vladimir would never in his lifetime openly support violent means, such as assassinations, for seizing power.

Despite the gains he felt he had made by reading and meditating so intensively, Vladimir was anxious to be reinstated at Kazan and to continue his education. Five months after he was expelled from the university, he made his first appeal to the authorities, but was flatly rejected. A letter by Maria Alexandrovna two months later had the same result, as did a request to go abroad for a while for health reasons. Finally, Vladimir's cloistered existence came to an end one year after it had begun, in the fall of 1888. Although he was still not permitted to re-enter the university, he was allowed to return to Kazan to live. And so, the Ulyanov family uprooted itself once again.

Maria Alexandrovna was very upset that Vladimir's once promising career now seemed to be in a permanent state of ruin. She continued to plead with the education officials, however, and even traveled to St. Petersburg to try to convince some of her husband's former co-workers to intercede on Vladimir's behalf. When nothing worked, she sold the property in Simbirsk that had been home for the Ulyanovs for so long, and bought a 225-acre farm near Samara so that Vladimir could try his hand at a new occupation—farming. But the nearest village, Alakayevka, was so tiny, so poor and run down that it did not even have a school of its own. In such a backward area, Vladimir found running an estate not at all to his liking. In order to get the work done, he felt that he had to put himself in the position of an evil exploiter of the rural peasants.

Luckily for Vladimir, his mother finally succeeded in making an arrangement for his further study of law before he had to hurt her feelings by quitting his work as a farmer. Maria Alexandrovna was not able to get her son re-enrolled in a university—the authorities felt that he would be a bad influence on the other students—but the Minister of Education granted Vladimir the opportunity to take the law examinations in St. Petersburg after independent study of whatever duration Vladimir saw fit. Systematic, detailed work was Vladimir's strong point. He buckled down to studying and, in just over a year, he assimilated all the required knowledge from the four-year standard course load. By November 1891 he had passed all the exams with perfect scores, and had received a university degree with honors.

Finally, Vladimir was ready to find a law firm in which to work. He was eventually taken on as a junior attorney at the offices of A.N. Khardin in the river town of Samara, not far from the village estate. Khardin was a liberal lawyer who had once played chess with Vladimir by mail while Vladimir was living in guarded seclusion at Kokushkino.

At twenty-one, Vladimir Ulyanov still had the sturdy, stocky build he had had from earliest childhood. He had never grown past medium height (five feet six inches) and his complexion was fresh and ruddy like his mother's. Yet Vladimir gave off an air of shrewdness and age beyond his years. His hairline was already receding, accentuating his large forehead, and a straggly reddish moustache and beard covered most of his face. His personality was such that he spoke little, and his piercing eyes and ironic smile often put people off. By 1891 he had been reading and brooding for four years. The death of his father, his brother's execution, and his own exile had changed him forever.

Despite all the hard work he had done to earn a law degree, Vladimir now had concerns that were more important to him than setting up a successful law practice in Samara. He was a revolutionary in search of a suitable location in which to carry out his work. He shared many of his brother's terrorist beliefs, all supported by his reading of Chernyshevsky and other revolutionary works. And he was starting to consider new philosophical terrain as well—the teachings of the German radical, Karl Marx.

Vladimir had read *Das Kapital*, Marx's major work, while in Kokushkino because he knew that at the time of his broth-

Lenin at age twenty-two, on the threshold
of his career as a revolutionary

er's execution, Alexander was planning to undertake a complete study of Marx's writings. In fact, by the end of the 1880s, Marx's written attacks on the "petrified" and "anachronistic" German state were being absorbed by most members of the Russian revolutionary movement. Marx preached that change had to come through revolution, not reform, and that revolution was imminent. It would come about through a fusion of philosophical thought and concrete action; when the progressive ideas of the revolutionaries ignited the masses of the country, a full-scale socialist revolution would take place, emancipating the masses. The segment of society that would provide the "material force" and hence the momentum of this revolution would be the working class, which Marx called the "proletariat."

Because Alexander died before he could make the transition from terrorist to full-blooded Marxist, and because Alexander's power over Vladimir's revolutionary thoughts was so great, Vladimir was reluctant to embrace Marxism wholeheartedly. He was not prepared to give up his faith both in terrorism as the best means of provoking political change and in the power of rural peasants (rather than industrial workers) to lead the revolutionary surge. Hence, in 1891— when the rains along the Volga never came and famine swept through Russia, when diseases like cholera and typhus reached epidemic proportions—Vladimir took a stand that was as cold-blooded as it was misguided. While Russian liberals and progressives converged in the Volga region in droves to provide relief aid, he stood by a basic principle of Chernyshevsky's thought: that the peasants would revolt only when their living conditions had worsened to the point of becoming unbearable. To Vladimir, the end justified the means and relief work seemed senseless. He scorned the efforts of the liberals to ease this situation, and he would scorn liberals in general for the rest of his life.

Samara was a provincial town with a population of around one hundred thousand. But, although it was a port on the Volga, it had no university, no cultural or social attractions to speak of, and no industrial working class. From the government's point of view, these characteristics made Samara the perfect remote location in which to isolate expelled university students and revolutionaries. From Vladimir's point of view these characteristics also made Samara a spot in which he could study the art of revolution.

Many former members of the People's Will organization lived in Samara at that time. They had grown older and had become alienated from the major cities in which they had done their conspiring. Their movement had thrived and then failed. Then along came Vladimir, the brother of one of their former heroes, and to his endless questions they were more than happy to give detailed replies. He wanted to know everything about their work: how they had joined the movement and in turn recruited other members; by what election processes they organized themselves and were led; what their philosophical platform was, how it was promoted, and how the masses responded to their overtures. Vladimir also questioned the radicals closely about their techniques for escaping from police surveillance, jail, and exile; how they established secret codes and passwords, obtained phony passports, and mixed chemical dyes and inks. He remembered everything that they told him, in case he needed to use the information at a later date.

Vladimir held the terrorists in high regard for their organizational abilities and techniques, but theoretically, he was starting to diverge from them. After he had learned all he set out to know, he pulled away from his People's Will contacts and began to spend more time studying Marx's writings and participating in Marxist discussion groups.

And then, in 1893, he began to write. His first project was a "book review" of a study by V.E. Postnikov on the rural conditions of southern Russia. The review itself was almost as long as a book, and by the time he was finished writing it, Vladimir had come to believe that capitalism existed in Russia (a prerequisite phase to revolution under Marxist doctrine) and that the industrial workers, not the peasantry, would be the class to lead the revolt. Vladimir made two copies painstakingly by hand for underground circulation and then read his work aloud to one of his Samara study groups. Since Postnikov's writings were not known in Samara circles, the essay's impact was all the more profound. Vladimir's reputation as one of the town's leading Marxists was established.

But the more Vladimir became involved in revolutionary work and the more he was convinced that the revolution would come from the industrial working class, the more Vladimir wanted to leave quiet Samara for one of the large industrial centers of Russia. He was prepared to become a full-time revolutionary. He had never had more than a handful of law clients and had never taken his practice too seriously. When his sister Olga died suddenly of typhoid in 1891, he had felt an obligation to stay near his mother to comfort her, but now, in 1893, he felt that the time was right for him to strike out in a new direction. A passport to go abroad, however, was again denied him, foiling his plan to go to Switzerland to meet with exiled Russian Marxists for an exchange of ideas. Instead, he traveled to St. Petersburg, the capital city of Russia.

WINDOW ON THE WEST

4

When Vladimir moved to St. Petersburg in the summer of 1893, it was the first time he had ever lived away from the Volga River. It was also the first time he had lived on his own, since the rest of the Ulyanovs left Samara when he did to relocate in Moscow. The new-found freedom was exhilarating, and in St. Petersburg Vladimir found himself in a revolutionary's paradise. The city had been built by Peter the Great to provide a "window on the West," the cultural and social link between Europe and Russia that would help modernize his vast but backward empire. The seat of government was in St. Petersburg, as were Russia's finest university and more than one hundred thousand of the nation's industrial workers. It was unquestionably the city in which a uniquely Russian brand of Marxism was taking shape and taking hold.

Vladimir situated himself in St. Petersburg under the flimsy guise of joining the law offices of another liberal lawyer, M.F. Volkenstein, who was more than happy to offer assistance to an up-and-coming revolutionary. Volkenstein never pressured Vladimir to take on a normal case load, and Vladimir made no pretense of supporting himself as a lawyer. In fact, he had no income in St. Petersburg at all because his scattered courtroom appearances were made in the capacity of public defender, for which no pay was forthcoming. He lived a spartan existence on money that Maria Alexandrovna was able to send from her modest pension, for by now, she was aware of Vladimir's intentions as a revolutionary and no longer tried to stand in his way.

Freshly arrived in St. Petersburg, Vladimir's most urgent business was to make his first revolutionary contact— Michael Silvin, a nineteen-year-old student who attended the St. Petersburg Technical Institute.

Silvin accepted Vladimir into the small circle of Socialist students at the Institute, and this signaled the beginning of a two-year period in which Vladimir would meet many of the key role players in his political future: close allies like Gleb Krzhizhanovsky, ideological opponents like Peter Struve, and Marxists with divergent viewpoints like Julius Martov. For the time being, though, in 1893, all of the Socialists were united in their underground struggle to bring about the all-important vision of Marxist revolution.

His St. Petersburg co-conspirators were unanimous in their lack of warmth or affection for their surly companion, but they were all eventually won over by his hard work, intense dedication to the cause, and invaluable practical sense. The group, which resembled scores of others in those years, called itself the *stariki* or "old men," even though all of its members were under thirty years of age. Their main activities consisted of writing papers on social issues in Russia, meeting to discuss politics, economics, and the works of leading Marxists, and, to some degree, creating and distributing Socialist propaganda to workers.

None of the revolutionaries were sure of themselves when it came to applying Marxist theory to the reality of the situation and undertaking the actual education of the industrial proletariat. The first steps taken were modest and cautious. Vladimir, like many of his cohorts, tutored individual workers and small workers' groups on the writings of Marx. His alias for this kind of activity was Fyodor Petrovich. Most

Sunday afternoons in 1894, for example, he would tutor a future revolutionary named Ivan Yakovlev by reading passages of *Das Kapital* aloud and then analyzing them in terms of their applicability to Russia.

Apart from the underground work being carried out by the Socialists, some aspects of the workers' education took place in a different kind of setting. Sometimes manufacturers took it upon themselves to create libraries or Sunday study sessions for their workers, often led by young liberal women from the educated class. The Socialists would attend the study groups and then work with the young women—without the manufacturers' knowledge, of course—to raise the revolutionary consciousness of the workers.

It was at one of these gatherings that Vladimir, soon to officially assume the name of Lenin, met his future wife, Nadezhda Krupskaya. Just before Lent begins each year the Russians traditionally celebrate Shrove Tuesday with a pancake festival. Such a party, which Lenin attended in 1894, was to be a front for a Marxist study meeting. No workers showed up that day, only revolutionaries, and their serious political discussion took place amidst frivolous decorations and traditional holiday foods and beverages so that any authorities who might happen to stop by would not be made suspicious. Krupskaya was impressed immediately with the newcomer's scornful remarks about some of the less successful aspects of the movement. She was one year older than he was, and looked the part of the liberalized turn-of-the-century woman, with short, bluntly cut hair and a carelessly put together outfit. She was thin and rather tall, with big eyes and a snub nose. When the party ended, Lenin walked her home slowly along the Neva River, which flows through the heart of St. Petersburg. They talked about their dedication to the revolution. Marxism would always provide the foundation and the centerpiece for their relationship. And Krupskaya would, soon enough, become an indispensable and dedicated part of Lenin's work as a revolutionary.

Lenin was very active in 1894. He created a study group from among Krupskaya's worker-pupils and initiated them into Marxism by reading to them from a simplified edition of *Das Kapital*, answering their probing questions, and interrogating them about their working conditions. He also wrote a series of three notebooks for underground consumption entitled "What are the Friends of the People and How Do They Fight Against the Social Democrats?" It was a lengthy defense of Marxism which took the oppositions' views to task one by one. *The Little Yellow Books*, as they came to be called, were soon established as underground classics, whose caustic style appealed to a wide cross section of revolutionaries and whose penetrating logic and thoroughness satisfied even the most academically-oriented of Socialists. None of the existing theoretical Marxist works were as comprehensive and practical, and none took such a hard-line tack. The high regard for the notebooks in St. Petersburg circles catapulted Lenin to the top of the revolutionary hierarchy. The recognition of his talents would only grow from there.

Slowly, the Marxists came to realize that their writing might actually have a decent chance of being passed by the government censors. In 1894, the same year that Lenin was distributing his notebooks through underground channels, Peter Struve succeeded in publishing a work on the problem of economic development. Suddenly it seemed as if Marxism had become legal. The revolutionaries were joyful but, naturally, puzzled by the government's newfound tolerance for them. Apparently, the authorities regarded the Marxists as rather ineffectual—all talk but no action. Other revolutionary factions, such as the terrorist organizations, posed much more of a threat. The government assumed that if they continued to stalk these more volatile "nationalist" groups, while encouraging the Marxists to make public attacks on the nationalists, they would have the revolutionary movement under their thumbs.

Lenin, like most other Marxists, decided to play along with the government's tactic. He immediately started to work on a book project and a journal that would have no problem passing into print. But he also began to prepare a manuscript, which would surely be censored, on how the government hoped to water down the revolutionary movement by creating a situation of seeming legality. And he continued to work hard in another area that the authorities as yet knew nothing about—the underground effort to redefine Marxism in terms of the workers' immediate needs.

Many of the Marxists had in fact realized, as the government had, that their struggle was not paying off in practical terms. The proletariat was simply not responding to the call to arms. Most workers were not particularly predisposed to politics, nor did they feel any urgent necessity to undertake the lengthy study essential to understanding Marxist doctrine. Yet without the cooperation of the proletariat, there could be no revolution, so the Marxists adopted a new approach. Rather than try to teach the workers abstract revolutionary theory and meaningless catchphrases like "Overthrow the autocracy!" or "Put an end to exploitation!" the Marxists decided to simplify the issues. Now, higher pay and improved working conditions provided the platform. Because labor unions were illegal in Russia, the workers had never been able to fight for such causes themselves; now they began to stir. The Marxists churned out mimeographed leaflets and underground newspapers (many of which were printed abroad and then smuggled into Russia) and distributed them in great quantities to the workers. The receptivity of the workers represented an important breakthrough, but much had yet to be done before revolution could come about.

In 1895, probably because of overwork, Lenin was bothered by stomach disorders and then he developed pneumonia. Maria Alexandrovna was so worried about him that she traveled from Moscow with a physician friend to see him. Lenin recovered and then used his illness as the excuse for finally securing a passport to go abroad. He had been turned down twice before, but this time the authorities granted their permission. It was common for revolutionaries to live outside Russia, away from the immediate repression of the czar's police, and the authorities now had little trouble guessing the true nature of Lenin's trip. They intended to watch him.

Lenin left Russia in April and set out not for the health spas of Europe but for the Swiss cities where the two founders of Russian Marxism resided in exile. First he went to Geneva to see Georgy Plekhanov, then thirty-nine, a brilliant philosopher who had once been a vital part of the "Land and Freedom" movement. Lenin was appropriately respectful and modest in the great man's presence. Plekhanov felt that the most urgent need of the revolutionary struggle in Russia was a strong leader of the proletariat, and he perceived in Lenin the makings of just such a man. For hours they talked of organization and ideology. Plekhanov's impression was, on the whole, very favorable, but he noted to himself Lenin's stodgy writing style, his lack of sensitivity to literature and the arts, and his intolerance toward the liberals. In the context of Lenin's life, there was no apparent reason for such animosity regarding the liberals; he had been born into a liberal family and the two lawyers who had saved his professional life by hiring him had been liberals. Yet he found the group as a whole to be a nuisance and not worthy of participation in the revolutionary cause. Plekhanov said to him, "We want to turn our faces to the liberals and you want to turn your back." But that was the only disagreement that the two men had at their first meeting. Plekhanov took heart that the practical side of the revolution might make great strides with the help of his young visitor.

From Geneva, Lenin traveled to Zurich to see Paul Axelrod, then forty-five, another patriarch of Russian revolutionary thought. Axelrod had not previously heard of Lenin, so their initial contact was short and uneventful. Lenin left a rare underground collection of Marxist essays with Axelrod overnight, and when he returned the next day, he found that Axelrod had been unimpressed with the manuscript except for an article by K. Tulin, which was one of the pseudonyms Lenin used in his writing.

Axelrod and Lenin spent a week together, debating the fine points of the article. Like Plekhanov, Axelrod was disturbed by Lenin's wholesale rejection of the liberals, and he worked hard to turn Lenin's opinion around. Finally, Lenin said that he gave in. By the time his visitor left Zurich, Axelrod was as convinced as Plekhanov that Lenin, with his theoretical abilities and organizational know-how, would be the one to lead the labor movement in Russia.

After four months abroad, including side trips to France and Germany to visit libraries and revolutionary contacts, Lenin returned home to Russia. The police, who had been keeping track of his whereabouts for more than a year, were ready for him at the border. They examined his trunk, even knocking on its false bottom under which a pile of illegal literature had been hidden, but they let him pass through customs. Then they followed him closely.

Lenin sensed that he was being shadowed, but he went about his business. It was the fall of 1895, and strikes were starting to erupt in and around St. Petersburg. Lenin and his group interrogated workers about their specific grievances, drafted proclamations and leaflets, copied them laboriously by hand or somehow arranged to have them printed, and then distributed them. In whatever spare time he had, Lenin trained his co-conspirators in techniques for setting up secret codes, making invisible ink, hiding documents and information, and dodging one's police shadow—the same methods he had learned from his People's Will contacts in Samara. In time the information would undoubtedly have proved useful, but an informer named Dr. Mikhailov had infiltrated the group, and, unknown to them, was relaying everything that he saw and heard to the local police.

The authorities finally decided to close in when an underground newspaper called *The Worker's Cause*, written and edited principally by Lenin, was ready to go to press. Most of the group members were arrested, and the others, including Nadezhda Krupskaya, were picked up later. When the group's contacts in the working class found out the identity of the police informer, Mikhailov was found murdered.

For the first time in his life, Lenin experienced prison firsthand. There he was to stay for fourteen months, in Cell 193 at the House of Preliminary Detention in St. Petersburg, while his case was under review. The jailers were not at all hostile to

Lenin is shown here with his fellow
revolutionaries in St. Petersburg,
around the time of their arrest in
1896. Lenin, who is seated at the
center of the photograph, is flanked
by Gleb Krzhizhanovsky on the left
and Julius Martov on the right.

the Marxist prisoners; rather they granted them various privileges because they did not expect such a scholarly group to be troublesome. Also, political prisoners had won a relative degree of leniency for themselves over the years by gaining public support for such desperate measures as hunger strikes and suicides. And so, Lenin's imprisonment was more like being trapped in a library than in a jail. Visitors were allowed in twice a week, and in the crowded and noisy meeting rooms it was easy to have open political discussions and to pass along fobidden reading materials. Books and journals were allowed in the cells, and soon Lenin's cell was filled with the bundles of reading matter that his mother and his sister Anna brought to him. He had everything he needed to carry on business as usual.

He corresponded with revolutionaries on the outside through Anna, who passed information to him in a miniature dot-dash code entered inside the books she brought. He made "inkwells" out of bread and, using milk as a sort of invisible ink that could be read when held in front of a light, he wrote the texts of pamphlets and statements between the lines of book print. Lenin also read books on economics and history and hundreds of journals, and he wrote articles for the legal press. To keep in shape, he did fifty sit-ups a day and chopped wood with the other inmates. He even played chess with men in neighboring cell blocks by signalling moves in a code that could be tapped out on the cell walls. From time to time, he was interrogated by the authorities, but he stubbornly refused to admit anything, even information that was undeniably true and for which the authorities held absolute proof.

From prison, Lenin maintained all of his connections and even engineered some strikes and walkouts. His involvement in the movement did not diminish in the slightest. Perhaps most important, he began to write his longest and most involved work, *The Development of Capitalism in Russia*. Lenin would lie in bed and plan out the chapters, but he had only partially completed the text in February of 1897, when he was informed that he was being transferred to Siberia for three years of exile.

Lenin never had a trial because, by law, the czar's police could sentence a prisoner to up to five years of exile without one. As the son of a government official with hereditary nobility, Lenin was allowed to travel to Siberia slowly and at his own expense. Before leaving, however, he renewed all of his revolutionary acquaintances in St. Petersburg and spent a few days with his family in Moscow. Then he wended his way by train and boat to the little village of Shushenskoye near the Yenisei River in eastern Siberia.

The province of Yeniseisk was probably the most pleasant possible place for Siberian exile. It was called "Siberian Italy" because of its relatively temperate climate. Other exiles, like Julius Martov, were often sent to towns that were hundreds of miles closer to the Arctic Circle—frozen, barren wastelands where it was hard enough to survive, much less study or write. Lenin realized his good fortune at once. The village had only fifteen hundred inhabitants, two of whom were fellow political exiles. He had much peace and quiet, and became stout on a hearty diet of mutton and dairy products. As he was not placed in one of the Siberian communities filled with exiles, he was, for the most part, spared police surveillance. Days were spent reading, writing, walking, hunting, and, in the winter, skating. The government provided a monthly stipend of eight rubles for lodging, food and other necessities. Lenin rented a one-floor wooden cottage with quaint but simple furnishings, and there he lived a settled, uneventful existence.

Nadezhda Krupskaya had been part of Lenin's group when it was broken apart by the police in 1896, but she had been allowed to stay at large for the eight months following his arrest. Then she too was arrested, detained for a while, and finally sentenced to three years of exile in the North Russian town of Ufa. Krupskaya filed two requests: that she be allowed to join Lenin, her "fiancé," in Shushenskoye, and that her sentence be lightened to terminate at the same time as his. The ruling was partially in her favor. She was told that she had to serve her full term, but it was permissible for her to

*Lenin's cottage in the Siberian
village of Shushenskoye*

spend all or part of it in Shushenskoye with Lenin, on the condition that they marry "immediately."

The relationship between Lenin and Krupskaya has always seemed curious. In St. Petersburg they had been dedicated and hardworking conspirators. From Siberia he had written letters to her that seemed affectionate on the surface, but were in truth laced with coded requests for information or for more reading material. When she wrote to tell him that she could join him in Siberia, he responded by sending her a list of books and periodicals that she should bring along. With crates and boxes galore, and with her mother, Krupskaya made the trip to Siberia. Lenin's landlord granted her and her mother the rest of the space in Vladimir's cottage. In July 1898, after a lot of official red tape, the marriage was performed locally in a traditional, Russian Orthodox manner. Atheists though they were, such a ceremony was the only legal way to get married in Russia then. For their honeymoon, Lenin and Krupskaya sat at home, translating Sidney and Beatrice Webb's *Theory and Practice of Trade Unionism* in the mornings and copying by hand the completed text of *The Development of Capitalism in Russia* in the afternoons.

Lenin and Krupskaya were to have no children, which was a great disappointment to Lenin, who had enjoyed growing up in a large family. And although there was not a lot of romance in their life together, they remained devoted to each other and worked well as a team.

With Krupskaya in Siberia with him, life for Lenin changed considerably for the better. Now he had not only a wife, but also a secretary, supporter, and housekeeper. He would never get along famously with his mother-in-law because, as a devoutly religious person, she objected to his atheism, and she defended her viewpoints unabashedly and often. But their banter was always clever and good-natured, and provided welcome comic relief. Krupskaya helped Lenin to increase his correspondence and improve the quality of his connections. The cottage became a sort of headquarters for all the exiles in the region, who would visit on one pretext or another and then stay for days or weeks. In addition to the constant turnover of guests, there was always a brisk exchange of books, journals, and newspapers.

Lenin's term of exile was coming to an end. In the last few months in Siberia, he sensed that the mood in Russia was shifting, but he felt powerless to understand fully how or to know what to do. In 1898 Socialists from all over Russia met in Minsk to discuss the future of the revolutionary movement. They drew up a manifesto that called for a renewal of People's Will tactics, this time to be carried out by and for the working class. They also set up what they called the Social Democratic party, but, unfortunately, most of the governing members were arrested and sent into exile before they could convene for a second time.

Revolution seemed further away than ever. And then, two nonrevolutionary schools of thought sprang up among Russian Marxists—economism and revisionism. Economism suggested that since the proletariat had grown so fast and the revolutionaries at large had become so few, all political struggle should be delayed while everyone focused on help-ing the workers to achieve their immediate goals of unioniza-tion, higher salaries, and better working conditions. The economists also wanted to work with the liberals toward establishing a constitution based on Western models. Lenin's repugnance for this point of view was exceeded only by his hatred for the other school of thought that deviated from mainstream Marxism, namely, revisionism. The revisionists wanted to abandon the revolutionary struggle altogether because they claimed that necessary allies like the middle class were being alienated from the movement and that with-out this support the goals of social reform and improved living conditions could never come about.

While all of this was transpiring, Lenin felt trapped in Siberia. He had lost his faith in the proletariat as the instru-ment of the revolution, just as he had previously turned away from the peasant masses. The workers were concerned only with their own immediate interests. And the Social Democrats, supposedly the political party that would lead the revolt, were falling into chaos and ruin. Lenin brooded constantly about the aberrations of the Social Democrats, and as a result, lost a lot of weight and sleep. Out of his inner turmoil, however, came the foundation for his own ideology, an ideology that would lead to the establishment of the Bolshevik party.

An essay in 1900 called "Urgent Questions of Our Movement" used the by-line of "V.I. Lenin" for the first time and identified the necessity of complete reorganization of the Social Democratic party. It had to be disciplined and trained in revolutionary technique in order to bring Socialist ideas and political awareness effectively to the proletariat. According to Lenin, a revolution would happen spontaneously within the proletariat only after a relatively small group of full-time, professional revolutionaries had succeeded in sufficiently raising the consciousness of the masses.

Obviously such an effort could not be coordinated from Siberia. Lenin—whose most recent alias was to stick—outlined a plan for setting up an official newspaper abroad for the Social Democrats of Russia. The paper, which would be smuggled into Russia, would not exist to report events or to provide a forum for theoretical debate. Rather, it would be a manual for the revolution—step by step it would instruct the Marxists of Russia how to proceed.

Lenin could not stop his planning long enough to eat or sleep. He corresponded with his former collaborators, Julius Martov and Alexander Potresov, who were also living in exile. Their terms of exile would end at the same time as his, and the three decided to meet in Pskov to make arrangements for going abroad.

In March 1900 the Siberian exile was mercifully over. Lenin and Krupskaya packed up as quickly as possible and began their long journey south. When they reached Ufa, Krupskaya could go no further because she still had one year of her term left to serve. Lenin left her and her mother there in the care of some trusted friends, and he continued on at once.

In Pskov, Lenin laid plans with Martov and Potresov for realizing his brainchild, a newspaper to be called *Iskra* or "The Spark." His request for a six-month passport was granted, but before he left for Europe, he became friendly with the radicals about town and approached them for funds for his new enterprise. The police, of course, were keeping tabs on all the newly-released revolutionaries. They watched with interest as Lenin and his comrades darted about, collecting money not only in Pskov, but also in cities such as St. Petersburg, Moscow, and Riga. These side-trips were illegal, because ex-prisoners were not allowed to travel freely. In May both Lenin and Martov were arrested in St. Petersburg with large sums of money. Surprisingly, not only were the two men released, but the authorities also seemed to believe their flimsy excuses and returned all the money that they had been carrying. After an argument with the policeman in charge, Lenin also got back his passport, and departed for Europe according to plan.

Lenin left Russia as a mature Marxist revolutionary. First in the seclusion of Kazan and Samara, then in St. Petersburg prison and Siberian exile, he had passed through his ideological apprenticeship. Now he stood at the forefront of a long, proud, and turbulent revolutionary tradition. While in Europe, he hoped to engineer nothing less than the successful culmination of that tradition—the overthrow of the czarist autocracy and the beginning of a Socialist utopia for Russia.

SPARKING THE FLAMES OF REVOLUTION

5

Lenin's dream of a newspaper that would unify and strengthen the Russian revolutionary movement became a reality on December 24, 1900. That was the day the first issue of *Iskra* was manufactured on a secret printing press operated by Social Democrats in the German city of Leipzig. The newspaper was modest in appearance—crowded lettering on small sheets of onion-skin paper—but it could not have been bolder in plan. Lenin's lead editorial in the first issue set the tone for his large-scale endeavor, and in it he outlined the basic themes that would characterize his political approach for the next few years.

Lenin perceived the main problem of the revolutionary movement in 1900 to be its fragmented nature. He called for leadership and organization of the kind that would bring all the factions together under one banner. Only then could the movement go forward toward revolution. In the absence of strong leadership, Lenin felt that the proletariat was losing its class identity, that the government's efforts to water down the underground activities and the industrial strikes were succeeding. To pull the workers together again, and to incite them to action, a new political party must be formed. From the head of the party, a small group of professional revolutionaries would educate the masses about their needs and interests, and would point them toward their goals.

In his editorial, Lenin stressed that broad political changes in Russia were imminent. The mood of the Russian people was so desperate that any single strike or revolt could have the potential to mushroom into revolution on a national scale. This view of revolution was no longer purely Marxist but showed some strong leanings toward the earlier Russian revolutionary viewpoints. It is interesting that Bakunin and his cohorts had felt this same sense of immediacy in the 1870s, and no revolution had come about. Lenin would find that revolution was close at hand, but not as close as he imagined.

Lenin's ideological flexibility would, in the long run, prove to be one of his strongest points as a leader. The political climate in Russia changed rapidly in the early years of the twentieth century, yet many of the Russian Marxists would not veer from their formula for revolution which had great applicability to the conditions in Germany, but less to those in Russia. At the same time, many of the radical viewpoints that were original to Russia, like those of the People's Will movement, became outmoded or had limited potential because they lacked a larger vision. In contrast, Lenin's training as a revolutionary had come from two vital sources—the Russian revolutionary tradition and the European Marxist tradition. His talent lay in knowing how to draw on both of these sources to evolve a view of revolution that had realistic possibilities for success in Russia. He was always mindful of the most current mood of the people and of the government. And, as evidenced by his skill at chess, Lenin had a talent for finding the best possible tactical move in any given situation. All of his writings in this period up to 1917 dealt with immediate, practical problems of the movement, and in 1900, the main problem was to unify and bolster the revolutionary movement, which meant the revolutionaries themselves as well as the masses.

Each issue of *Iskra* provided Lenin with a fresh opportunity to get his viewpoint across, and most of his early articles did just that through open attacks on economism and revisionism, the two movements derived from Marxism that Lenin perceived as a real threat to the revolution. But the newspaper could never achieve its purpose if it did not get into the hands of a very large proletarian audience. With the help of the Social Democrats in Germany, Lenin had only minor difficulties producing the paper. But the main hazards of the enterprise lay in smuggling it over the border and then distributing it to the right people on the other side. For this task Lenin had an elaborate plan.

The newspaper was printed in Leipzig and then shipped to Berlin, where it was stored in the cellar of the German Social Democrats' headquarters. There the issues were folded down into small squares and concealed in false-bottomed trunks and shipping crates that were transferred to towns near the Russian border. The most crucial links in the operation were the professional smugglers, who managed to get the papers into the hands of *Iskra* agents at various points across the border in Russia. Officials in both Germany and Russia were constantly trying to spot the exchanges so that they could dismantle the network, and over the years, many of the smugglers were caught and sent into exile in Siberia.

But the enterprise continued, and it was, on the whole, quite successful. The *Iskra* agents distributed their newspapers to contacts among the intelligentsia and the workers, who would in turn organize readings and pass the materials along. When the newspapers wore out from being passed around so much, word of mouth carried the message further. Copies of *Iskra* were scattered on the streets, pasted on walls, sent through the mail. Sometimes, bold *Iskra* workers would even shower theater and concert audiences from the balconies with papers when hall lights had been dimmed for performances.

At first, the leaders of the reading circles and the *Iskra* propagandists in Russia tended to be students enrolled in high school or the university, with no practical knowledge of revolutionary tactics. But slowly, procedures and warning systems developed so that, as Lenin had planned, a band of revolutionary leaders started to emerge.

The Russian authorities were relentless in their attempts to isolate and stamp out the revolutionary forces. Cossacks would often crash in on meetings or come thundering on their horses after street propagandists. The proponents of *Iskra* led dangerous lives, but not so, Lenin. In Munich, he rented a small room in a saloon under the name of Meyer and lived very frugally. He was relatively safe there, with no immediate fears of being discovered and arrested. Although he felt guilty about placing his workers in more danger than himself, he rationalized that the mastermind of the operation must stay removed from the arena of action.

In April 1901 Krupskaya's term of Siberian exile was over and she left Ufa to find her husband. Once they were together again, Lenin and Krupskaya rented a tiny, crowded house in the suburbs of Munich. Krupskaya brought stability to her husband's life-style and working habits, as she had when she joined him in Siberia a few years before. She discouraged Lenin's close friend and collaborator, Julius Martov, from spending so much time with Lenin each day so that he could devote more hours to writing. She took over all of the housekeeping chores as well. On their daily walks, Lenin would tell her about what he had just written and she would comment and criticize. Most important, she took responsibility for overseeing the underground network of *Iskra* agents and smugglers, freeing Lenin to spend the bulk of his time on writing and publishing *Iskra*.

Because the owner of the Munich printing plant would no longer agree to turn out copies of *Iskra*, the editorial board of the paper voted to move to London in the spring of 1902. Once there, Lenin was dismayed to find that his understanding of written English did not help him to get around in England. The spoken language completely baffled him at first, so he "studied" it by attending endless meetings and lectures, and sitting in pubs and buses so that he could watch the mouth movements of British and listen to them closely. Both Lenin and Krupskaya took to London, with its close, quiet streets and bustling working class.

The year 1902 also marked Lenin's publication of what is often considered one of the most important works of the twentieth century, *Chto Delat?* or *What Is to Be Done?*

The title was borrowed from Chernyshevsky's radical novel of the 1860s, which Alexander Ulyanov had read so carefully and which Lenin had savored time and time again while on his reading binge in Kokushkino. Lenin added to his own essay the subtitle, "The Burning Questions of Our Movement." Although its significance was not apparent immediately, *What Is to Be Done?* presented Lenin's blueprint for the party organization that would, in time, succeed in bringing about revolution. The 1902 essay turned around the basic principle of Marxism that revolution will erupt spontaneously within the working class when it can no longer contain itself and lashes out at its miserable living conditions. Instead, Lenin made the case that the workers' consciousness can only be raised to the point of revolution with the help of forces that exist *outside* their downtrodden existence. He saw the workers not as the instigators of the revolution but more as its material. From their isolated expressions of unhappiness with their lot, it was up to a political party of all the consolidated revolutionary factions in Russia to mold the belief among the proletariat that the entire ruling system must be discarded. The only party that could tackle this feat in the face of the czar's secret police force would be a small group of conspiratorially trained, professional revolutionaries.

Lenin had touched on this notion of a small, secret group of revolutionaries in his earlier *Iskra* editorials, but never with such strength or depth. Now his powerful new theory stood in stark contrast to the mainstream of dissent. Most of the other schools of revolutionary thought, including Marxism, advocated wresting the power from the czar and handing it directly to the people rather than placing it in the hands of another individual or group of individuals. Lenin, however, understood that mass revolt in Russia was not shaping up according to

Marx's theory. Instead, the potential for revolution was being systematically undermined by the authorities. The only possible success, Lenin believed, would result from implementation of his plan. It was a purely practical approach. It was his style to deal only in immediate, practical issues. Lenin left only one issue rather vague—how to govern in the aftermath of the revolution when the time came.

The publication of *What Is to Be Done?* received a mixed reaction from the editorial board of *Iskra*, which was composed of all of Lenin's closest conspirators. While he had put forth most of his ideas already in issues of *Iskra*, never before had he so openly presumed to redefine the Marxist mission for Russia. To the other editors, Lenin's essay represented a theoretical cry of independence. There could be no doubt that Lenin intended to be the leader of his brainchild, the revolutionary elite. His philosophy was so transparently self-centered that it could not be construed as anything other than a personal bid for power.

Lenin could never have hoped to launch *Iskra* or unite the revolutionary movement without help from Plekhanov, the mentor whom he had sought out in Geneva a few years before and who was now among his co-editors. But he had begun to feel constrained by Plekhanov's "orthodox" brand of Marxism. After *What Is to Be Done?* appeared, they started to quarrel. Lenin's dry writing style had never pleased the literary-minded Plekhanov, and now it became the subject of a round of bickering. When the party program came up for discussion, a full-blown argument ensued. The two men raged bitterly at board meetings over who should be targeted to carry off the revolution—the proletariat alone (as Lenin believed) or the proletariat and the more conservative lower middle class (as Plekhanov believed). The board's attempts at compromise were scorned by Lenin, who would not budge from his beliefs, and the rift between Plekhanov and Lenin only grew worse.

Despite Lenin's vehemence and stubborness on the surface, all of his internal tensions and frustrations started to mount and to take their toll. He became more and more intolerant of those with whom he worked closely. Plekhanov seemed to him haughty and thin-skinned. The others seemed wishy-washy or apathetic, softened by middle-age, by their underground lives, or by years of subjugation to the Russian penal system. Lenin had built *Iskra* to unify the movement, but what he saw at the board table was just more fragmentation. Not even the six editors could agree on standard party procedure. Lenin refused to give in on anything. And he boiled up inside each time he was forced to defend his principles. In future years, when his power was secure, Lenin would only preach, he would never argue.

In the midst of all this disenchantment with his associates, Lenin was truly impressed by a new acquaintance. Very early one October morning in 1902, a loud triple knock—the signal among the revolutionaries—came at Lenin and Krupskaya's front door. Krupskaya, still wearing her nightgown, rushed downstairs to let the visitor in before he woke up the other tenants. It was Leon Trotsky, a Social Democrat who was only twenty-three years old, but who had already made a mark on the revolutionary movement. His fearless behavior had earned him the nickname "the young eagle," and his florid writing style, the nickname "the pen." He was fresh out of Russia, having just escaped from exile in Siberia.

Trotsky (whose real name was Lev Davidovich Bronstein) was penniless. While Krupskaya paid for his cab, he rushed upstairs where Lenin was still in bed and immediately engaged him in animated conversation about the *Iskra* organization. Trotsky was especially concerned that Russian underground groups discontinue their own papers and support *Iskra*. Perhaps because Lenin was going through such a difficult time with his co-editors, he was particularly taken with Trotsky, and the two men became fast friends. Lenin introduced Trotsky to the *Iskra* staff and tried to get him elected to the board. Plekhanov, however, stood in the way, judging Trotsky to be too brash as a man and too flowery as a writer. He undoubtedly realized that Trotsky's appointment would tip the balance of power on the board in Lenin's favor. Without a unanimous vote, Trotsky could not be elected, and Plekhanov readily provided the veto. Nevertheless, the young man dedicated himself to the *Iskra* effort and soon became an integral part of the organization.

In April 1903 the editorial board voted five-to-one to move *Iskra* to Geneva, because most of the members no longer wanted to live in London. Lenin cast the only dissenting vote. He was afraid that in Geneva, Plekhanov's home turf, the paper would fall more under Plekhanov's control. All of the tensions that had been building up in him since he first ventured abroad came crashing down on Lenin. Normally he was very healthy, but now he became quite ill and spent his first two weeks in Switzerland in bed. When he got back on his feet again, he had regained his fighting spirit, and was ready to make his first serious power play.

His opportunity came in the summer of 1903, when *Iskra* called a meeting of all the Russian Social Democratic factions. Such a convention had been held in Minsk in 1898, but only a minimal amount of theoretical groundwork had been accomplished before the leaders were arrested, thereby undermining subsequent meetings. Out of respect for the 1898 organizers, the 1903 meeting was called the Second Party Congress. The delegates were to rendezvous in Geneva and then proceed to Brussels together.

Everyone anticipated a showdown between Lenin and Plekhanov. But as the delegates arrived one by one in Switzerland from Russia, no rifts were immediately apparent. Lenin was extremely excited about the prospects for the congress. He tried to anticipate all the issues that were bound to come up, and talked personally to each delegate, trying to sound them out and win them over.

In July 1903 the forty-three delegates moved to Brussels, where, to avoid the police, they were forced to hold the Second Party Congress in various locations, mostly trade-union halls and warehouses around town. The major personalities—Georgy Plekhanov, Vladimir Lenin, and Julius Martov—at once revealed themselves. Plekhanov spoke gracefully and eloquently to the gatherings, attracting followers as he had for the past twenty years with his noble vision and elegant demeanor. He had been waiting for this occasion for a long time and intended to make the most of it. Lenin, now thirty-three, had an equally significant impact on the group, but his style was completely different; his strength lay in his simplicity and directness, qualities that the delegates (many of them workers) could easily understand and rally behind. For Lenin this was the occasion for making a move to achieve greater power over the revolutionary movement. Martov had been Lenin's closest collaborator, from the St. Petersburg underground circles through arrest and Siberian exile, and then the frenzied creation and governing of *Iskra.* He looked poor and untidy, with baggy clothes, a straggly beard, soiled glasses, and a stooped gait. But his words gave him a strong appeal since they revealed a high intelligence and a fierce dedication to the revolutionary cause.

Plekhanov opened with a stirring address that called for the unification of all the rival groups within Social Democracy. He stressed the need for a single labor party, ruled by a coherent program and a constitution. The delegates in the rat-infested hall cheered and wept, while the police observed the proceedings from just outside. After only four or five meetings, when nothing of substance had yet been decided, the Brussels authorities singled out four delegates and told them to be out of town within twenty-four hours. The congress reconvened in London, again in union halls. And there the bitter arguing began.

The problems arose over the terms of the party program because the delegates' ideological differences were substantial in some areas. The three major factions to disagree were the *Iskra* representatives, the economists, and the Jewish Socialist Bund (a group made up of Jews from Russian Lithuania, Poland, and central or White Russia that sought cultural, political, and social solutions to discrimination against them). The economists were not ready to yield any of their hard-earned ground to the *Iskra* organization, and the Bund members came out immediately against a tight, centralized party system. Lenin was after a high degree of discipline within the party, with himself at the helm. Of the *Iskra* group, Martov represented a strong democratic force that had to be eliminated if Lenin's plan was to succeed. Lenin advanced a hard-nosed motion to set up a presidium of three men— Lenin, Plekhanov, and a man named Pavlovich-Krasikov—all from the *Iskra* faction. Martov, predictably, disagreed with Lenin. He felt that such a presidium was undemocratic, that a nine-member presidium representing all the dissenting factions would be more appropriate. Plekhanov forgot his differences with Lenin long enough to cast his support for the three-man presidium, reasoning that this dictatorship—a "dictatorship of the proletariat"—was necessary to bring about the order needed for democracy. Lenin's motion was passed, and Lenin would later comment that it was important to have "iron-fist" control over the party. The disagreement with Martov was just the first signal of the upcoming total break between the two men.

On the next issue—party membership—Martov came out the victor. Lenin insisted that to qualify as a member of the party, a person should not only subscribe to the ideas of the party but also actively work in one of the party organizations toward realizing the overall program. He wanted a core of true, participating revolutionaries. Martov saw the necessity for admitting anyone who believed in the program into the ranks of the party, and he won the congress over to this viewpoint by a vote of twenty-eight to twenty-three.

That was Lenin's only loss, however, and with each vote Lenin drew closer to achieving his goal of a small revolutionary elite. Plekhanov, an unwitting pawn in Lenin's subtle power play, backed Lenin throughout the meetings. Their consolidated energies made them an invincible team. First they won a motion for a tight party organization, against the wishes of the Bund for a loose federation under which some of the individual Social Democratic groups' autonomy could be preserved. Then they succeeded in dissolving all the independent factions and officially combining them into one party. At this, the Bund contingent and several other groups withdrew from the congress and walked out in a fury. Finally, Lenin succeeded in paring down the editorial board of *Iskra* from six to three members: Martov, Plekhanov, and himself. The three who were cut from the board—Paul Axelrod, Alexander Potresov, and Vera Zasulich—had all been Martov supporters. Trotsky and the former *Iskra* board members realized that Lenin was trying to take over and attacked him publicly at every opportunity. But it was too late; Lenin's coup was now almost complete.

Plekhanov lent his invaluable support to one more of Lenin's crusades. He made a crucial speech that put the importance of the revolutionary goal above the need for organizing the revolt democratically. In effect, he made a case for anything that would further the cause of revolution, including, conceivably, terrorism and a revolutionary elite. "The health of the revolution is the supreme law," he reasoned. "If the safety of the revolution should demand the temporary limitation of one or another of the democratic principles, it would be a crime to hesitate." Plekhanov's words drew cheers as well as cat-calls. Lenin was aglow. He would quote the speech often over the next fifteen years, particularly around the time that he actually took over the new revolutionary government of Russia. Plekhanov, on the other hand, soon regretted his words. Realizing that he had overstated his case, he readdressed the congress in the hope of impressing upon the delegates that he was not recommending his view as a standard revolutionary procedure, but rather as a last resort. Unfortunately, the damage had already been done. Plekhanov was pegged as a full-blooded Leninist.

By the time the congress ended, anything but unification had come about. Lenin had succeeded in permanently alienating many of the Social Democratic factions and in seizing the leadership role for himself. Trotsky and Martov, who had been Lenin's two closest friends and collaborators before the meetings, now categorically opposed him. And Plekhanov was beginning to realize that he had been used by Lenin as a means of consolidating power. Lenin's followers in the congress came to be known as the Bolsheviks (from the Russian word *bolshinstvo* for "majority"), while Martov's followers earned the title of Mensheviks (from *menshinstvo* for "minority''). These labels became permanent, and the two factions continued to oppose each other. In the coming years, Lenin would attack the Mensheviks on the ground that they were merely philosophers, that they never acted on their convictions. In actual fact, the Mensheviks shared the same ideological goals, but their methods of bringing about change were vastly different. The Mensheviks, true Social Democrats, sought to educate the proletariat slowly and improve working conditions through trade unions. They felt that it was too early to seize power from the czar because Russia was not ripe for revolution. The Bolsheviks, on the other hand, desperately endorsed action; immediate results were their very banner and creed.

Back in Geneva, Plekhanov made a move that he hoped would bring the party back together again. The three-member editorial board of *Iskra* had been reduced to two members because Martov had resigned out of anger. Now Plekhanov proposed to go back to the six-person board, reinstating all the editors who had either left or been eliminated. This time Lenin refused, and when Plekhanov expressed his insistence, Lenin resigned from the board. ''It is impossible to work with the Mensheviks. You will see,'' he fumed. Thus, the tie between Lenin and Plekhanov was irrevocably severed. Lenin had made a bold move, and now he was obliged to follow his convictions on his own.

To outsiders, Lenin now seemed cold and hard. He was self-assured to the point of being bull-headed. He rarely joked and, when he argued, it was with a vengeance. He was fanatical about the revolution; for him, there were only two kinds of people, those for it and those against it. He once told a friend that anyone against the revolution should be put in front of a wall and shot. At the same time, he scarcely concealed a hatred for those revolutionaries who opposed the Bolshevik outlook.

On the inside, though, Lenin retained some of his softer qualities. He was as devoted as ever to his wife and his family. The tensions of the Second Party Congress left him drained and worn, and the summer of 1904 saw him on the verge of a nervous collapse. Krupskaya insisted that they spend some time together in the Swiss countryside. They hiked from Geneva to Lausanne, Interlaken, and Lucerne, taking plenty of time to swim, sleep, and gaze at the snow-capped mountains and crystal-blue lakes. After a month, Lenin felt strong enough to return home to Geneva and lay his next round of plans.

One of his first moves was to set up another newspaper, a competitor to *Iskra* that was to be the true rallying post of the revolution. Lenin won over a Marxist writer named A.A. Bogdanov, and through Bogdanov he enlisted the help of several young Russian Marxists-in-exile to help prepare the paper. Gradually, he was able to assemble a full-sized staff of twenty-two Bolsheviks, including a former chess partner from Siberia. Lenin called the new paper *Vperyod* or "Forward," and appointed an editorial board of seven to assist him. Naturally, this time around, Lenin retained supreme editorial control himself. But he did not have much to worry about. The newspaper was a fast success, and the editorial board worked together in perfect harmony. Lenin's spirits picked up considerably.

Lenin's Bolsheviks were as yet a small group despite the fact that they had represented a "majority" at the congress. But the dedication of his co-workers gave Lenin hope; indeed, they were highly respectful of him. As the paper began to be well known in the revolutionary circles of Europe and Russia, people began to refer to him as "Ilich," his middle name, which for Russians is an expression of familiarity and yet veneration. He never intended for people to make him a hero or to idolize him, but he did not fight the new image. Anything to further the cause of revolution.

In the years from 1900 to 1905, while Lenin was seeking to take over and advance the Russian revolutionary movement from his position abroad, conditions in Russia were slowly degenerating into chaos and anarchy. For the superstitious peasants, the czar's very coronation in 1894 provided the first hints of the empire's impending doom. Nicholas II, descended from the Romanov family that had ruled Russia for three hundred years, became the czar when his father Alexander III died unexpectedly. In fact, he and his German wife

Alexandra Fyodorovna were married in the very bedroom of the dying czar, earning her the nickname of "the funeral bride" among the lower classes. At the coronation of Nicholas and Alexandra, a huge St. Petersburg festival turned into tragedy when more than two thousand peasants were trampled to death in a field where the rumor had spread that the food was running out.

By the turn of the century, it was obvious to more than just the simple, superstitious folk that the new czar would do nothing to improve the lot of the masses in a period of mushrooming industrial activity. Nicholas ruled Russia in the same outmoded autocratic manner as his father's line before him. Personally, he was a gentle, distrustful, indecisive man who tried to counter his own instability by pretending to be quite sure of himself. He insisted on having total authority over Russia and allowed no popular elections of government officials, no courts, no parliaments, no freedom of the press. Nicholas could choose to heed or to ignore his advisers. He was suspicious of the terrorist groups that had claimed the lives of his grandfather, Alexander II, and so many other figures in authority. The only person he absolutely trusted was his domineering wife, Alexandra, whom he dearly loved. He often relied on her to make political decisions for him, and over the years she increasingly based the advice she gave him on the irrational mystical beliefs with which she guided her own life.

The czar had good reason for his suspicions. Even with his administration's harsh repressions, the underground tide of socialism was spreading and threatening to rise up in a surge. No longer could the dissent be pinpointed in one or two small, self-contained revolutionary groups. Apart from the Social Democrats, who were struggling to incite revolution through the proletariat (and out of which evolved Lenin's Bolshevism), other important movements existed. The Social Revolutionaries operated on the assumption that the peasants were the rightful owners of Russia's land; they sought to shift the power through terror and their assassins claimed many victims. Another group, made up of anarchists, was rather incoherent about its aims but also used terror to achieve its ends. In this case, however, only the czar and his immediate advisers were targets. Finally, the Constitutional Democratic Party, or Kadets, formed among the liberal intelligentsia, stood for the establishment of a democratic parliament somewhat like England's.

The line of distinction between revolutionaries and the rest of the population became ever vaguer. Outside the cities, peasants rebelled quietly by cutting timber for themselves and harvesting crops for their own consumption, in violation of the rules. In the industrial centers, the number of strikes and demonstrations multiplied and dissent became bolder as workers jammed public squares, attacked policemen, and fought back when fired upon. At the universities, strikes sprang up again, and members of the liberal intelligentsia—professors, doctors, lawyers—made their voices heard. The czar's forces were as ruthless as ever, beating and murdering to squelch the riots and the subversive behavior. But their tactics no longer worked. The masses had been riled, and their brute force had the obvious potential of overrunning and destroying the czar's unstable perch at any moment.

In February 1904 Russia found itself at war when Japanese submarines fired on the Russian fleet. The revolutionary forces at home stood still momentarily and patriotically rallied to the cause. But the czar and his advisers mismanaged the war effort. Russia's forces in Japan held out for eight months and then succumbed to siege, anarchy, and starvation. The country could not mobilize its cumbersome army quickly, so the army suffered one defeat after another. By the time the forces were finally ready for competitive battle, the revolutionary temperament in Russia had grown so disgusted and outraged with the motley military display that it redoubled its rebellious activities. The czar sensed that his empire would crumble if he continued to wage war, so he sent an ambassador to the United States to negotiate a compromise with Japan. He would need all his power to stave off an onslaught by his own people.

The anticipated uprising flared in 1905, led by a curious revolutionary figure named Father Georgy Gapon. Gapon was a thirty-two-year-old priest of Ukrainian peasant stock who had convinced the Russian authorities that he should be involved in the police's early efforts at unionizing the workers. The theory behind the legal police unions was that they might channel off some of the revolutionary fervor, and Father Gapon seemed a harmless choice as a "spiritual supervisor" for such a group. He created a "Union of Russian Factory Workers" in St. Petersburg in 1904 for the purpose of improving working and living conditions for the workers, organizing group activities, stamping out drunkenness and gambling, and spreading religion and patriotism. The workers were predictably dubious about the new organization at first, but after Gapon was judged to be sincere, they flocked to him in droves. Soon thousands of St. Petersburg workers had signed up as union members.

Father Gapon did much to undermine the hatred and bitterness for the czar that such a large percentage of the workers harbored. He praised Nicholas for legalizing their efforts to raise the level of their existence. He had the workers sing "God Save the Czar" at all their meetings. And when a group of metal workers at the Putilov locomotive shops staged a walkout, he concurred that general workers' grievances should be presented to the czar himself. Father Gapon's faith in Nicholas was naively placed, however. Carried by the impetus of his union's needs, he went over the heads of his superiors in the police department and the Ministry of the Interior to write a note to the czar that announced a workers' pilgrimage to Palace Square the following day.

At 2:00 P.M. on Sunday, January 9, 1905, more than two hundred thousand workers and friends assembled near the Winter Palace, unarmed. They formed a quiet procession, many of them holding traditional icons and pictures of Nicholas. At the head of the group marched Father Gapon, carrying a scroll. The text on the scroll conveyed four messages: the workers were oppressed and wanted to respectfully ask for better pay and working conditions; the government levied taxes and became involved in detestable wars with no acquiescence from the people; the people should be given the right to vote and to elect representatives to a Constituent Assembly; and they would die to defend these requests.

The orderly congregation marched slowly and silently across the snow-covered square toward the czar's palace. But Nicholas had left St. Petersburg with his family at the first sign of trouble for a "vacation" in the south that would last eight months. Hundreds of armed troopers waited outside the palace in his place. They closed in on the ranks of the marchers and shot to kill. Soon the snow had turned red with blood. According to estimates, at least five hundred men, women, and children lay dead, while around three thousand more were injured. Those who could escape did so in a hurry, then returned later to cart off their dead kin. The day was called Bloody Sunday. Never again would peaceful protest be a viable program for change in Russia; never again would the czar be trusted.

News of Bloody Sunday reached the revolutionaries in Switzerland quickly. Martov, who rarely slept, was told in the middle of the night. Trotsky discovered the headlines in the early morning paper that lay outside the *Iskra* offices the following day. Lenin and Krupskaya found out from co-workers at *Vperyod*, who intercepted them as they were walking to the Geneva library.

Most of the revolutionaries-in-exile were ecstatic, convinced that their long-awaited moment had come. The Bolsheviks gathered at a local restaurant and sang the Revolutionary Funeral March with great emotion. But Lenin proceeded to the library. He was not convinced that the revolution had at last come.

His letters to Russia in the next few weeks were tentative in tone because he was unsure of the situation there. But instead of devouring statistics as he had been doing on his daily trips to the library, Lenin switched over to studying books on street fighting and war strategy. One by one the other revolutionaries were able to smuggle themselves back into Russia with the youngest and the hardiest going first. The twenty-five-year-old Trotsky, not surprisingly, led the pack. But Lenin was in no particular hurry to go anywhere. He waited until a general amnesty was granted in October, and only then did he start his journey back to St. Petersburg.

REVOLUTION

6

The news that reached Europe about the events of Bloody Sunday and its aftermath was often vague and confusing. That was because the situation, even to those at the heart of the action in Russia, was constantly in a state of flux. The czar's uncle, also the Governor General of Moscow, was assassinated by the Social Revolutionaries in February 1905. A union of unions, composed of liberals and radicals, was formed in May and demanded a parliamentary government. In August the czar granted a mock concession—the formation of a Duma, or popular assembly, which would advise him on political matters but which would hold no legislative powers. All of this time and into the fall, a wave of strikes and protests persisted and soon it seemed to engulf the whole nation. By October a general strike had halted railway transportation throughout all of Russia.

But that was not the full extent of Nicholas' troubles. The Mensheviks, led by their hero Trotsky, had rushed to form a central strike committee with the Social Revolutionaries in St. Petersburg. It was named the Soviet of Workers' Deputies, and within a few days of its creation, the new organization was plainly so potentially powerful that the word "soviet" became a new possibility for a government alternative. A mere forty worker-delegates represented the twenty thousand St. Petersburg factory workers at the first few meetings, but the result was a dramatic call for the proletariat at large to join in striking with the railway people.

By offering a coherent course of action for the angry masses, the Soviet was able to harness itself to the chaotic backlash after Bloody Sunday. Now its members hoped to provide new impetus for the revolution. At the end of October, strikes had paralyzed every facet of daily life—factories, shops, telephone and telegraph services, electricity, schools, and restaurants. The czar had no choice but to give in. He endowed the Duma with the constitutional rights of free speech and assembly, the legal power to organize labor, and greater freedom to appoint its own members. Furthermore, the Duma's approval was made a requirement for the passage of all new laws. But Trotsky was not satisfied; he called for the strikes to go on.

And so they did. Then, on October 31, a huge demonstration sponsored by the Soviet was brutally broken up by sailors and police who were loyal to the government, as well as by the notorious Black Hundreds, private vigilante groups sponsored behind the scenes by the czar's secret police. The strikes were crushed, but the revolutionary newspapers continued to demand shorter working days, higher wages, and a true constitution free of czarist control. In early November, another general strike was sparked by a mutiny among sailors at the Kronstadt fortress. This time, because the influence of the Soviet had spread to all layers of the society, the army was somewhat sympathetic to the workers' cause. The authorities put down the strike with difficulty.

At this point, Lenin arrived back in Russia. He was surprised to find that the strikes and the violence were so widespread; perhaps the revolution was imminent after all. But he was dismayed that the Soviet of Workers' Deputies was already so well formed. Lenin wanted revolution, but he wanted it on his own terms. The Soviet, made up loosely of

Mensheviks and Social Revolutionaries, did not fit Lenin's ideal of a tight organization composed of a handful of professional revolutionaries. Yet the Soviet was already so widely accepted among the workers that it was a strong force to be reckoned with.

The Bolsheviks disappointed Lenin greatly during this time. He chided them for not having been prepared to further their cause when the strikes first began, but he was at a loss to explain precisely what they should have done. Instead he lectured the underground Bolshevik groups on warfare tactics, like making bombs, using different kinds of arms, and killing policemen. Eventually, he came around to the outlook that a complete rejection of the new Soviet was not wise. He used the Bolshevik newspaper in St. Petersburg, *Novaya Zhizn,* as the vehicle to advocate his new theory: that the Soviet was not encompassing enough, and should be expanded into a more viable provisional government for Russia.

But the initial surge of the 1905 revolution was slowly being neutralized. Throughout the country, the spontaneous and often poorly organized protests were persistently crushed. The Black Hundreds went on a campaign of terror in which thousands were killed. And the czar, even behind the back of the premier he had appointed to negotiate with the workers, moved to regain his full powers. On December 16, a demand by the Soviet for a tax boycott and the formation of a Constituent Assembly was received with indifference by the beaten-down masses; nevertheless, as soon as the radical demand was published, the czar had all the members of the Soviet's executive committee arrested.

But if workers in St. Petersburg had become apathetic to new revolutionary demands, workers in Moscow were still receptive. Lenin himself was in Finland then, but when a general strike started in Moscow, the newly-trained Bolshevik fighting brigades rushed into action. They threw up barricades and distributed leaflets instructing people how to group together and fight. The revolutionaries took hope when the workers managed to hold their own against the police for more than a week. But then, in one fell swoop, a division of the czar's artillery crushed the rebellion, ending the "revolution."

Only the Duma remained as a tangible result of the revolt. Several revolutionary groups, including most notably the liberal Kadet party, thought that it showed promise for eventually establishing a constitutional rule. But most of the radical groups—the Bolsheviks, Mensheviks, Social Revolutionaries, anarchists, and others—considered the newly-formed Duma a sham. In 1906 the Kadets won a majority of seats on the new Duma, mainly because the other radical parties boycotted the election. Lenin, predictably, despised the Kadets because he had no tolerance for liberals in his political life. He called them down publicly for agreeing to sit and negotiate with the very powers who had created and continued to reign over a brutal police state. However, the Duma went into effect and Lenin's outcries did nothing to undermine support for it. The Bolsheviks did not enjoy much popularity in the revolutionary ranks in 1906. Their desperate display of guerrilla warfare during the Moscow uprising had not gone unnoticed; in fact, it had earned them an unsavory reputation as unreasonable, cold-blooded terrorists.

Lenin's Bolsheviks began to insist that he smooth things over by making peace with the Mensheviks. A secret congress for the purpose of achieving unity was arranged to take place in Stockholm, prior to the first assembly of the Duma. Lenin had agreed publicly to go along with the majority rulings of the congress, and after all was said and done, unity was indeed established—on Menshevik terms. Lenin did not expect this defeat, because he thought he had won over enough of the delegates to sway the vote in his favor. However, his participation in the congress had been a calculated move. He had planned to use the consolidated powers of the two groups to undermine the Duma had he won the majority vote, but he did not consider himself bound in any way by the decisions of the congress should they not meet with his personal approval.

Back in Russia Lenin resumed his attacks on the Duma. The secret police did all they could to encourage these attacks, since the czar understood that a powerful Duma might actually succeed in siphoning off some of his power. In the meantime the Duma convened and drafted a petition demanding various reforms, including political freedom, an end to capital punishment, equal rights for the ethnic minorities, and democratic rule of the local governments. The czar stalled as he tried to size up exactly how much support the Duma had among the general population.

Finally the government found its excuse for doing away altogether with the bothersome Duma. Lenin had organized Bolshevik contingents of sailors and soldiers to insist publicly that the Duma stop making speeches and actually get some results. These groups were closely watched and heavily infiltrated by members of the secret police, and when one of these illegal military groups approached Duma members with a list of revolutionary demands, the police were ready. They closed in on the meeting and exposed the military group's petition. The Duma deputies present were charged with high treason, and in June 1907 the Duma was officially dissolved. New elections were to be held in six months, in which the Bolsheviks would decide to take part and would win representation.

Once the Duma was temporarily out of the way, the police had no further use for the Bolsheviks. Realizing that his days of freedom were numbered if he stayed in Russia, Lenin made an impromptu nighttime escape across the icy Baltic Sea to Sweden with the help of some Finnish peasants. He had realized long before that the true revolution had not yet arrived. Now it was time to retreat and to lay new plans.

The year 1908 found Lenin back in Geneva, starting his revolutionary work from scratch. His paper, once called *Vperyod* but now renamed *Proletari* or "The Proletarian," occupied most of his time. He had to build up the entire editorial operation again and then go through the tedious business of creating a new smuggling network. It seemed as if the whole movement had suffered major setbacks, or, worse, as if the past few years of hard work had been for nought.

In fact, most people judged that Lenin was finished altogether. He was a hunted man. The czar had regained all of his

old powers in Russia, and, what was more, he had appointed a fairly competent prime minister named Stolypin who understood the need for aiding Russia's economic development and building a middle class. Many of the revolutionary supporters, particularly among the liberal intelligentsia, turned away from the underground struggle and went back to their former jobs as lawyers, professors, and doctors. And the workers, on whom Lenin pinned all his hopes, scaled down their revolutionary activities. Compared to the total number of striking workers in 1905, only 26 percent were active in 1907, 6 percent in 1908, and 2 percent in 1910. The nine years from 1908 to 1917 would be a long haul for Lenin, a test of his strength and endurance. The scandals that he faced along the way would almost break him. But he would persevere.

Lenin had renewed his participation in Social Democratic activities and had pledged at a party congress in London in 1907 to put an end to the armed units that he had formed for the purpose of engineering uprisings. But he had never given the actual order for those units in Russia to disband. On the surface Lenin still supported party unity and he even held the major representation in the Central Committee. Behind the scenes, however, he worked deviously to promote the Bolshevik ideology as powerfully as ever.

Lenin's main concern was financial; he needed to raise enough money to keep the Bolshevik cause alive. Donations from wealthy supporters like writer Maxim Gorky, millionaire Savva Morozov, and rich engineer Garin-Mikhailovsky were just a beginning. He needed much, much more. In desperation, he got involved in some shady dealings.

*Lenin's fund-raising
efforts took him to Italy
to visit the wealthy Russian
writer, Maxim Gorky. Here he
enjoys a game of chess with
a fellow Russian while Gorky,
wearing a hat, looks on.*

Scandals erupted. First Lenin was linked to a stage-coach holdup in Tiflis in 1907 (engineered by a man named "Koba," later to be called Stalin). Soon after, he was identified as the organizer of a counterfeiting operation, and was barely able to stay in the good graces of the party by quickly destroying the evidence.

Lenin fell into an acute depression in late 1908. He studied in the library by day but spent most evenings attending productions at the local cinema or theater just to escape his barren room. Unable to concentrate, he and Krupskaya walked out of most of the movies and plays before they ended. His only revolutionary activity during this time was the preparation of underground newspapers like *Proletari.*

In 1909 he moved to Paris with Krupskaya and with their dwindling resources rented a large, sunny apartment, which was shared with Lenin's sister Maria and Krupskaya's mother. But his luck only changed for the worse. Lenin's state of apparent poverty made it difficult for him to get the required endorsement from his landlord in order to be able to borrow books from the local library. On the bicycle that he used for transportation, he got into several minor accidents with cars. And finally his bicycle was stolen from its parking space on the porch of the house next door. Lenin was in poor health. He was run-down and pale, plagued by sleeplessness and terrible headaches. And he was burdened by the realization that he had many enemies. At a congress of the Socialist International held in Copenhagen in 1910, Lenin was attacked by practically all the other factions present as the main force behind the party's inability to unify. Back in Paris a dissenting group went so far as to raid the cafe where the Bolsheviks habitually congregated and started a brawl. Lenin escaped unharmed, but he was so upset by the incident that he wandered through the streets of Paris in a haze until the sun came up.

Still Lenin refused to compromise with his opponents in the party. The main point of contention in 1911 was the attitude toward trade unions in Russia. The czar's prime minister, Stolypin, had overseen the passage of a law which stated that unions were legal as long as they stayed out of the political sphere. The Mensheviks rushed to support this new government measure. But Lenin saw it as a trap and predicted the "liquidation" of the party if the revolutionaries took the bait.

Lenin had only two faithful Bolsheviks—Gregory Zinoviev and Leo Kamenev—by his side to help lead the cause. They would remain true to Lenin until long after his death. Together the three men launched a new revolutionary newspaper in St. Petersburg called *Zvezda* or "The Star," dedicated to keeping the underground spirit of the movement alive. At first influential names like Plekhanov contributed articles, but after a while they dropped out because they preferred to advocate the legal avenues of reform. *Zvezda* became Lenin's personal podium for spreading the Bolshevik philosophy.

Then, in April of 1912, the political calm in Russia was shattered. When the leaders of a gold miner's strike in the northern Siberian town of Lena were arrested and the workers objected, hundreds of strikers were gunned down by government troops. A rash of industrial strikes broke out spontaneously across the country. The czar's forces quickly extinguished the disturbances with arrests and more violence—even Stalin was caught in St. Petersburg at *Zvezda* headquarters and sent into Siberian exile—but the temper of the times could not be so easily quelled. Once more Russia was in a revolutionary mood.

Lenin seized the opportunity to initiate a legal daily labor newspaper in St. Petersburg called *Pravda* ("Truth"). To this day, *Pravda* is the major newspaper in Russia. Such a grand-scale project was made possible at the start by the vast resources that Lenin had built up through his shady financial dealings. The Mensheviks, by contrast, could only afford to produce a small weekly paper, despite their larger following among the unions. *Pravda* caught on at once, particularly since it avoided mention of the squabbles between Socialists. Promoting itself as the cornerstone of a united workers' movement, *Pravda* reported on all important labor activities, including personal accounts of factory disputes and texts of speeches by Socialists in the new, re-established Duma. The newspaper's success prompted Lenin and Krupskaya to move to Cracow, Poland, so they could be as close to the Russian border as possible. From this position, they could reduce the difficulties of editing and of orchestrating Bolshevik activities from abroad.

After a few months of renewed popularity, Lenin decided to ease back into his old habits. He held a Bolshevik committee meeting in December 1912 where it was decided that underground demonstrations and strike provocations would be resumed by Bolshevik organizations in Russia. In August 1913 a Central Committee meeting of all the Socialists provided the opportunity for Lenin to push through his resolution that Bolshevik and Menshevik representation in the Duma should be officially split. The Mensheviks in the Duma were outraged, because they had not been consulted. Attacks on the Mensheviks became sharper and more frequent from Bolsheviks sources. *Pravda* hurled insults at the Mensheviks at every opportunity, and as the Bolsheviks began to win the support of several of the large unions in Russia, a wave of arrests of leading Mensheviks began. The Mensheviks leveled charges that Lenin's top representative in the Duma was a police agent; Lenin denied the accusation in *Pravda,* but the Duma member refused to appear before a tribunal and resigned hastily from his party post.

The Social Democratic party was in tatters. When the International Socialist Bureau tried to intervene to establish party unity at a conference in Brussels in 1914, Lenin and his cronies Zinoviev and Kamenev refused even to attend the meeting. Plekhanov, Martov, and other Russian Socialists accused Lenin of stealing property that belonged to the party at large and of sheltering secret police agents in his organization. They called for Lenin's power in the party to be reduced so that unity could at last be established. The International was at a loss as to how to proceed, however, since Lenin was not present at the meeting, and his stand-in Bolshevik representatives refused to discuss the matter. Before any concrete steps could be taken, Russia went to war against Germany and Austria.

Involvement in World War I turned out to be Czar Nicholas II's biggest mistake. In 1914 Russia was barely getting on its feet in terms of industrialization. It was far outclassed by all the other major powers involved—England, France, Austria, and Germany—in the area of arms production. The transportation systems were not well enough mobilized to handle heavy wartime shipments of armies and grain. The peasants were as oppressed as ever, and the bureaucracy as stubbornly incompetent.

Yet at first, the Russian war effort was successful and the revolutionary movement faded into the background. Patriotism ran high, even among the liberals, who joined the fighting forces in droves, and among the peasants, who believed that by fighting countries with a higher standard of living than Russia, they could assimilate wealth and ideas that would help them to raise their own standard of living.

In July and August of 1914 the Russian army went on the offensive abroad, sweeping into East Prussia to drive back the Germans, and into Carpathia to demolish the Austrian and Hungarian forces. In western Europe, however, Russia's allies could not hold their own. The Germans crashed through Belgium and France. When the taking of Paris seemed imminent and an invasion of England was just a matter of time, powerful Russia, with its string of victories, provided the Allies' last hope for salvation.

But in the autumn of 1914, Russia's fortunes in the war turned for the worse. Through an inexcusable tactical blunder that left an attacking army without backup, the Russians lost 170,000 men in the battle of Tannenburg in the German countryside. In the constant fighting that ensued, the Russian armies lost around thirty thousand men a day because the arms ran out and the food reserves in the homeland could not reach them through the broken-down railway system. By November Russia had managed to save France from the German offensive, but Austrian gains had been speedily reversed. The suffering and starving Russian soldiers fell not only into hopeless disrepair but also into bitter resentment of the czar and, finally, into anarchy.

Indeed, the czar's tentative understanding of his country's situation was slipping away completely. He relied heavily on his wife's intuition for making his major political decisions;

and, unfortunately, since 1905 she had been under the influence of an odd mystic named Rasputin. A peasant from western Siberia who claimed to be a "man of God," Rasputin had won the czarina's faith by successfully predicting that she would bear a male heir to the throne after she had borne four daughters. He had also used his "powers" to improve little Alexis' health when it seemed that the royal son was going to die from his hereditary illness of hemophilia. In 1914 Rasputin had warned against Russia's involvement in World War I, and by ignoring the advice of his wife and Rasputin, Nicholas did in fact get himself deep into trouble. In late 1914, with the Russian army withering from isolation, malnourishment, and a string of defeats, Alexandra and Rasputin advised the czar to dismiss the commander of the Russian forces and to take charge himself.

Nicholas went along with the idea. By taking up command at war headquarters on the front and devoting all his time to military matters, he was able to stabilize the forces in 1915. But this left the internal affairs of his country totally in the hands of his wife. Scandals piled up in the administration, and dozens of police and cabinet officers, both competent and incompetent, were relieved from duty daily. By 1916 the country was falling apart at the seams—inflation was out of control, there were serious food shortages in all the major cities, and the mood of the people was decidedly against the incompetent czar and his wife. In the fall of 1916 all strata of society revolted. Coups were planned from inside the nobility; the Duma decried the government's policies publicly; and the peasants and workers started to strike regularly again. Although he was under pressure from all his advisers to do something about the situation, the czar would not take any measures to reverse the tragically miscalculated judgments that the czarina had made under Rasputin's influence. He took advice only from his wife, who told him to be strong and to continue as he had been doing.

On December 16, 1916, Rasputin was murdered by members of the royal family who felt that they could no longer stand by and watch the disaster. Nicholas and Alexandra were virtually alone. It was apparent to everyone, including the royal couple, that the mood of the country would not simmer much longer before a major revolt of some kind erupted. For the time being, though, the masses were without revolutionary leaders. All of the organized movements in Russia had been crushed and their leaders had been sent to jail, into Siberian exile, or into exile abroad. If the masses were to rise up, they would have to do so spontaneously on their own.

Abroad, in Switzerland, Lenin had always been against the war. When it was first declared, he angrily proposed that the new revolutionary slogan become "Turn your guns on your officers!" By appealing to the latent patriotism of the Russian people, Lenin feared that the government would succeed in undermining not only the revolutionary leadership but also the revolutionary spirit in Russia. He hoped that the masses would have the foresight to turn the continental war into a Russian civil war. He attacked any and all Socialists who supported the war effort as it stood.

At first Lenin was an outcast. Most of the revolutionaries abroad followed the logic of Plekhanov, who felt that German militarism posed the greatest immediate threat to their movement, and that Socialists of all the Allied nations should band together to insure its defeat. The Russian revolution could wait. Lenin debated bitterly in public with Plekhanov on this point, arguing that a war of and for the ruling classes should not be allowed to undermine or delay the revolutionary struggle. The war should be transformed at once into a battle between the proletariat and the government. As it became apparent that this situation would not come about, Lenin placed his hopes on Russia's losing the war so that the revolutionary spirit could be re-established.

In September 1915 Lenin spoke in Zimmerwald, Switzerland, at a conference for all the European anti-war, revolutionary groups. He raised a militant cry for open civil war and the creation of a revolutionary International. Even in this setting, his pronouncements met with a cool reception. The delegations from the various European countries were so entrenched in their individual struggles against their governments that they could not stop squabbling long enough to reach a consensus on anything. After the conference almost broke up with no results, a very loose anti-war Socialist organization called the Zimmerwald Union was formed. It was not quite what Lenin had in mind, but it would remain in force until after the Russian revolution had taken place and the Communist International had been formed.

Lenin's political unpopularity did not stop him from developing his revolutionary ideas further. In early 1916 he believed that revolution in Russia could only come about under the auspices of a dictatorship of the proletariat as well as the peasantry. Previously he had put all his faith in the power of the proletariat to revolt. But, while he still felt that the proletariat should lead the revolution, he realized that its successful culmination was impossible without the help of the peasants, to whom would fall the task of overthrowing the entrenched system of landownership. The proletariat, by carrying out its main responsibility of leading the Russian war effort, would eventually succeed in spreading the spirit of Socialism (with its core philosophy of equal rights for all) across the European continent, thereby triggering revolution in other countries as well. That was a strong reason for bringing about the revolution in Russia as soon as possible, even before the war had been terminated by the czar.

In 1916 lack of money forced Lenin and his wife to turn some of their attention to the struggle of daily living. Efforts to find free-lance writing and editing work were a failure. They moved to Zurich in January and rented a tiny room in the apartment of a former hotel cook from Vienna, where they were obliged to eat all their meals with the professional criminals and prostitutes who also lived in the apartment. Finally they could stand it no longer and took a more expensive room in the house of a shoemaker who was sympathetic to the underground movement. Lenin liked the man so much that he refused to move again, even though the rent was more than he could afford.

But there was not much about life in Zurich that was pleasant for Lenin. Inciting revolutionary activity from abroad was increasingly difficult, especially when the tide of revolutionary opinion was so set against him. He never took to the life of an exile and avoided contact with other members of the community of Russians there. In 1916 he was also greatly upset by the death of his mother, to whom he had been devoted and whom he had not seen since 1910.

Yet return to Russia meant certain arrest and Siberian exile, and so Lenin persisted in his revolutionary work abroad. At a second Zimmerwald Committee meeting, he managed to push through one of his resolutions to censure the International Socialist Bureau for its "pacifist" attitude toward the world war in progress. But the victory was minor, and, as there was no outlet for positive action, Lenin began a period of intensive writing again. He worked on a new book called *Imperialism, The Highest Stage of Capitalism,* which expanded Marx's ideas from *Das Kapital* to encompass industrial capitalism on a world scale. Lenin wrote that capitalist states would inevitably seek to expand beyond their present limits in order to continue growth and to establish monopolies in the world economy. In seeking out new markets and colonies, wars between these powers were inevitable. The wars could be circumvented only if the entire system of capitalism were obliterated. Revolution was more likely to develop in countries where capitalism was in its beginning stages, rather than in the more highly developed capitalist nations. The task of revolution fell to the Socialists, who needed to use violence in order to succeed. Only after violent upheaval took place could a peaceful world situation be established.

The book won Lenin no apparent new support, though. He was, instead, more unpopular than ever, and many were convinced that he had even gone mad. As the war dragged on interminably, a destitute, depressed Lenin lectured any small workers' group that would listen. He spoke of the "grave-like stillness" of Europe and the seething, underlying revolutionary spirit. But as late as January 1917 he did not sincerely believe that the revolution actually would come about for quite some time, maybe not even in his lifetime. And then, all at once, it happened.

Late in February 1917 the dam burst. The shortages of bread and wood had grown more serious than ever before because heavy snowfalls and bitter cold had cut off the already feeble national transportation systems. In Petrograd, as St. Petersburg had been renamed, workers flowed from the factories into the streets to line up at the bakeries. Crowds soon overran the city, shouting and looting stores. For the first time, Cossack troopers were in sympathy with the workers, so no violent actions were taken against the strikers. Only after the work walk-outs and transportation stoppages had totally paralyzed the capital, and most of its 2,500,000 people had filled the streets, did the czar's ministers realize that their hour of defeat had arrived. They cabled the czar, who was at his headquarters in Mogilev and was concerned primarily with the war effort and his childrens' case of measles. The czar sent back strict instructions to his ministers to quell the rioting within twenty-four hours.

But it was too late. A Cossack touched off the violence by shooting and killing a mounted policeman in Petrograd's Znamenskaya Square. That set off violent incidents throughout the city over the next few days, and on February 27, a crowd invaded the infamous Litovsky Prison and burned it to the ground. The few remaining loyal troops were gunning down demonstrators, while the secret police continued their futile raids on supposed revolutionaries. The Duma held an emergency meeting but was at a loss to know what to do. The Council of Ministers realized that they were utterly powerless. By this time, the crowds were so out of control that they were destroying every symbol of the czar's power that they could find. Tens of thousands of people marched to the Tauride Palace, where the Duma, the only alternative to the czarist regime in sight, had convened. One by one, factory spokesmen and regiment commanders proclaimed their allegiance to the Duma. Finally the members of the Duma rose to the occasion and, in the incredible absence of all revolutionary leaders, announced that they agreed to undertake the establishment of a new government and a new social order for Russia.

The czar, again underestimating the situation, headed back to the capital city from Mogilev in his imperial train. He had recalled some of his troops from the battle lines to retake control of Petrograd in his name, but they could not arrive in time and none of the Petrograd regiments could be counted on. As he traveled toward the capital, he decided to accept a constitutional monarchy, but it was far too late for that. By March 2, two Duma representatives had been dispatched to meet the czar's train and to demand that he step down from the throne. The czar finally realized the hopelessness of his situation and abdicated on behalf of himself and his young son, Alexis.

Before the factories had shut down, most of them had named representatives to a Soviet, the kind of workers' organization that they had hoped would take over in 1905. Most Soviet representatives in 1917 were Mensheviks and Social Revolutionaries. Now the Executive Committee of the Soviet and the Duma Committee worked together to appoint members of a provisional government, to go into effect immediately after the czar's abdication. Their first act was to convince Nicholas' younger brother, the next Romanov in line for the throne, that he should not try to assume power. Fearing for his life and realizing the futility and extreme unpopularity of the royal system, the Grand Duke Mikhail went along.

The next set of tasks would be much more difficult for the provisional government: to give the Russian people civil rights regardless of social class or religion, to elect a Constituent Assembly that would set up the new form of government and a constitution for Russia, and to oversee democratic elections of government officials on the local level. They also determined that amnesty should be extended to all political prisoners and exiles, that the national militia should replace the police, and that freedom of speech, press, assembly, and strikes should go into effect forthwith.

The popular hero to emerge from these proceedings was Alexander Kerensky, a thirty-six-year-old lawyer who served as minister of justice in the provisional government as well as a member of the Executive Committee of the Soviet. Kerensky had come from Simbirsk, like Lenin, and his father had been the school director who had played so important a role in Lenin's education. The young Kerensky had won his reputation in political trials, particularly in his defense of the

Lena gold mine strikers in 1905. A member of a small group close in philosophy to the Social Revolutionaries, he had become a leader of the moderate Socialist wing of the Duma and a champion of labor causes there. Handsome, articulate, and possessing boundless energy, Alexander Kerensky won a large following as the turbulent events of the revolution unfolded around him. His speeches were bold, fiery, and eloquent enough to impress the radical Soviet, the moderate Duma, the seething masses of factory workers, and the unruly soldiers who had deserted and were on their way back from the front. He proclaimed the suffering in Russia over, saying that peace throughout the world was the next goal for all. Under the banner of "liberty, equality, fraternity," a new age of freedom would reign.

The spirit of Russia's newfound freedom infected more than just the participants of the revolution. From all corners of Siberia, from prisons throughout the land, and from locations in Europe and as far away as America, the jailed and the exiled revolutionaries started their excited pilgrimages home. When Lenin's good friend Bronsky told him what had happened in Petrograd, he was shocked at first, suspecting that it was a plot the Allies had engineered to prevent the czar from independently establishing a treaty with Germany. He insisted on reading the news himself in the Zurich newspapers before he could allow himself to believe it. Then, panicked that the revolution would run its course without him, he set about finding a way to return to Russia as quickly as possible.

Stalin got back first. Returning from Siberia with some other former members of *Pravda*'s editorial board, he used his seniority to take over the newspaper's operations at the end of March 1917. *Pravda* had stood opposed to the new provisional government, in keeping with the Bolshevik philosophy that the only true revolution was a revolution led by the party. But Stalin, moved by the energy of the times and completely out of communication with Lenin, reversed the paper's policy. He came out cautiously in favor of the provisional government and editorialized about the possibility of unity with the more radical Mensheviks and some other Socialist groups. This new line was acceptable to many moderate Bolsheviks and was met with glee by the opponents of the party, but it puzzled and infuriated many Bolsheviks who wanted to adhere strictly to party policy. As for Lenin, he refused to give an ideological inch. And when his first postrevolutionary editorial was finally published in *Pravda* on April 3, the middle-of-the-road approach to Bolshevism was heard of no more.

For the time being, though, Lenin's major problem was to escape his isolation in Switzerland and find a way back to Russia. The new provisional government was not attempting to keep him out, even though they realized that he opposed them. But the war was still going on and the Allied British and French authorities, uneasy about Lenin's anti-war stand, hesitated to grant him visas to travel through their countries. Finally Berlin provided a solution. Germany had always sought to undermine the Allied war effort by encouraging Russian revolutionary activity, and these efforts were now helped by a man called Parvus (Dr. A. Helphand)—a Russo-German, who had been expelled as a Social Democrat and suspected of war profiteering and spreading subversive propaganda in Russia. Through Parvus, an agreement was reached; Lenin and several close comrades would be transported through Germany to Russia in a "sealed" train.

The plan was carried out quietly and in great haste. Because the Petrograd Soviet had not been consulted and so never granted its approval, Lenin not only broke the law but also drew the epithets of Socialists in all the Allied nations for colluding with the enemy. As the train left its Swiss station for Berlin, a group of anti-German Socialists cried out, "Spies! German spies!" Lenin brazenly looked out the window at them, shaking his head and smiling. A fist fight broke out on the platform.

Through Germany, Sweden, and Finland, the train moved along on its high-priority mission, disrupting rail schedules all the way. Lenin gazed out at the scenery he doubted he would ever see again and questioned his companions until late into the night about the details of the Petrograd coup. In Stockholm Parvus tried to set up a meeting between himself and Lenin to discuss a possible alliance with Germany, but Lenin would not oblige, explaining that he was a revolutionary, not a statesman. Parvus did meet with one of Lenin's comrades on the train, Karl Radek, and it is suspected that the two men struck some kind of a deal.

From Tornio, Finland, Lenin sent a telegram to his two sisters, Maria and Anna, that read simply, "Will arrive Monday at 11 P.M. Tell *Pravda*." He could not be sure what to expect when he got to Russia. Perhaps the members of the provisional government had changed their minds and intended to have him arrested as he tried to cross the border. But the train entered Russia without incident and Lenin grew happier and more excited with every passing mile.

A few hours before it was to reach Petrograd, the train stopped to pick up several Bolshevik leaders to brief Lenin on the situation in the capital. When Lenin saw Leo Kamenev, one of his closest collaborators, his first words were, "What have you been writing in *Pravda?* I have been calling you all sorts of names!" But the words were spoken with good humor and affection, not with harshness. The party on the train swarmed around their comrades from Petrograd and plied them with questions on the new government, the mood of the people, and the status of law enforcement.

Finally, on April 3, the train pulled into Petrograd's Finland station. A brass band played the French "Marseillaise," because they had not yet been able to learn their new anthem, the Russian "International." Bolsheviks of various ilks—sailors from the Kronstadt fortress, members of the workers' militia, and the Red Guard (made up of Petrograd workers)— lined the platform. Two hundred Bolshevik delegates marched into the station in formation. Lenin and Krupskaya stepped from the train amidst cheers and were engulfed by the happy crowd. Everyone present at the Finland station that evening expected great things from Lenin. But, probably, no one suspected just *how* significant he would be in shaping their lives and the future of their country.

VICTORY
AND
BEYOND

7

The Lenin who arrived at the Finland station on April 3, 1917, was forty-six years old and as set in his mission as ever. It seems inconceivable that this man, whose following probably numbered around two hundred thousand at the time, was able in eight short months to take over as supreme ruler of Russia's entire vast population (around 150 million). Lenin played the tumultuous events of that era by ear, and in retrospect, he almost always knew just when to take a firm stand and when to retreat. The real roller-coaster ride of the revolution took place in those months after the czar abdicated his throne, and after the struggle was over, the victors stood to inherit more problems than Nicholas II had ever dreamt of.

Lenin made his goal perfectly clear as soon as he stepped down from the train at the Finland station. To the soldiers, sailors, and workers who awaited a speech, he said, "I do not know as yet whether you all agree with the provisional government, but I know very well that when they give you sweet speeches and make many promises they are deceiving you, just as they deceive the whole Russian people.

The people need peace, the people need bread, and the people need land. And they give you war, hunger, no food, and the land remains in the hands of the landowners." Lenin's call for peace, bread, and land would become his standard cry. He implored the Bolsheviks to rise up and fight a world revolution in the name of the Socialists, a revolution in which the proletariat would triumph. At the official greeting ceremony held for him at the station, Lenin repeated his message, completely ignoring the opening remarks of Comrade Chkeidze, who asked for unity among the revolutionary parties. The Bolsheviks listened to Lenin, astounded. Since they had not had access to Lenin's most recent writings and since *Pravda* had been supporting the provisional government thus far, they had no idea that their leader would take such a radical line.

From the Finland station, Lenin was escorted to the palace of the famous ballerina Mathilde Kshesinskaya, which had come to serve as Bolshevik party headquarters after the czar-supporting Kshesinskaya had been forced to move away. Bolshevik orators excited the gathering crowd by making speeches from a second-floor balcony. From time to time, Lenin himself would go outside to announce his new themes: that the provisional government must fall, that the war must end, and that an international revolution must begin. In a two-hour speech given late that night in the mansion to key party workers, Lenin spoke like a man obsessed, explaining his thoughts. He supported regional people's councils, or soviets, as the proper form of government and said that they should take over the leadership of the country and draft new laws. "All power to the soviets" was his new slogan. Lenin further declared that the provisional government was ineffective and should be done away with completely. And he felt that, since the so-called Social Democrats had not supported the true cause of the workers, the Bolshevik party should be renamed "Communists." As for the peasants in the countryside, they should seize the land from their landowners as they saw fit. When Lenin finished defending his points, the audience applauded him enthusiastically. But it would be

An artist recorded Lenin's arrival at
Finland Station in a style characteristic
of Russian revolutionary art.

some time yet before Lenin could manage to convert their cheers into concrete action.

Lenin had a good point about the provisional government; its ineptness was responsible for an escalating situation of anarchy in Russia. By not ending Russia's involvement in the war, the ministers were remaining loyal to England and France and were holding out against the monarchy in Germany. But the Russian defeats on the German front had demoralized the nation. Supplies and arms could not be produced fast enough and so never reached the armies, and a decree passed by the Petrograd Soviet took away the right of commanders to punish their soldiers or to order them to act against their will. With no clothes, food, weapons, or ammunition, and with no disciplinary action to fear, the troops became so disillusioned and disgusted that desertion crippled the ranks. Thousands of peasant soldiers left for home daily, until the army was depleted by two million soldiers. Among the fifteen million remaining, bitterness and anarchy were rampant.

Within Russia itself, the atmosphere was also increasingly one of turmoil. Because the interim provisional government did not move quickly to organize popular elections for setting up a Constituent Assembly to rule the country, a situation of "dual power" involving the provisional government and the soviets developed. At the head of the provisional government, Kerensky, now minister of defense, was single-minded in his determination to win the war. He used the most powerful means at his disposal—his own eloquence. Kerensky traveled around tirelessly at the front, delivering impassioned speeches to the haggard troops, and he actually did boost morale quite a bit. But as the war dragged on and the defeats continued, the figure of Kerensky soon became synonymous with the failure of the provisional government to bring peace. Popular opinion was on the side of the soviets, which held no official governing power, but which had been created by popular vote and therefore more accurately reflected the feeling of the masses. Since the provisional government and the soviets often disagreed on policy, they cancelled out each other's effectiveness. In the face of the paralysis of the ruling powers, the people started to take matters into their own hands. Peasants in the countryside pillaged the estates of the landowners with greater and greater frequency, while city workers rioted for food and took over their factories.

Lenin knew that the time was almost ripe for a civil war, and he tried to consolidate his power in the ravaged country as quickly as possible so that he could lead an armed insurrection at just the right moment. In the confusion of 1917, Lenin found that his decisive new program held a lot of appeal. He focused on spreading his ideas for solving the present national crisis, rather than on spending his time defiling Kerensky, the Mensheviks, and the Social Revolutionaries. The Mensheviks, Lenin realized, were so split in their opinions and so ineffectual in power that they would eventually undermine themselves.

During these months, Lenin's ability to express popular aspirations in such pithy slogans as "peace, bread, and land" gained him much ground. But probably the single most important factor that ultimately made Lenin invincible was his collaboration with Leon Trotsky. Trotsky returned from exile in America in May (he had been publishing a Socialist newspaper in Brooklyn, New York) and took charge of a party of "interfaction" Socialists who had become estranged from both the democratizing Mensheviks and the dictatorial Bolsheviks. Trotsky, despite the personal slanders he had suffered from Lenin and the Bolsheviks over the years, soon realized that in the revolutionary current only Lenin had the potential to bring about actual results. He was also drawn to Lenin's insistence on international revolution, the conviction that Russia would ignite a proletarian Socialist struggle that would spread throughout the world. For Lenin, a hard-headed intellectual with an aversion to speaking publicly before the masses, the fiery Trotsky was an invaluable cohort. Trotsky provided the flashiness and eloquence that the Bolsheviks had been lacking. He never tired of riling up the crowds with heart-felt, exhilarated oratory, and his popular appeal was enormous. Within a few weeks of his return to Russia, Trotsky was second in command of the Bolshevik party. The close collaboration between the two men would last until Lenin's death, although Lenin would always safeguard his own supreme power in the party by limiting Trotsky's political responsibilities.

In June 1917 the character of the revolution began to change. As the revolutionary factions struggled against each other with increasing openness and finally violence, the high hopes for national unity and the formation of a new democratic government were dashed. Kerensky tried to save his popularity by launching a major offensive of the southwest army under General Brusilov, but, although the move succeeded at first, the Russian army was eventually driven back by the Germans. Lenin in the meantime planned at least two large-scale street demonstrations, neither of which actually materialized, and it has never been discovered if Lenin meant to use them to engineer his coup. Then, in July, while Lenin was staying at a cottage in the Finnish countryside for a rest, an uprising spontaneously erupted in Petrograd, with thousands of workers and soldiers marching through the streets, demanding immediate action in terminating the bumbling provisional government and Soviet.

On July 4, when Lenin arrived in Petrograd, huge crowds were milling around the Bolshevik headquarters and heckling all speakers who tried to quiet them down. Word arrived that twenty thousand Kronstadt sailors were on their way to join the mobs. At first Lenin thought that the time for revolution might have arrived. But the Soviet quickly turned the tables on Lenin by calling in loyal troops to control the crowds, by destroying the *Pravda* presses, and by taking over the palace that the Bolsheviks occupied. Warrants for the arrests of Lenin, Trotsky, Zinoviev, and Kamenev went out, with Lenin accused of acting as a German spy. Lenin had indeed been receiving money from the Germans to back up his revolutionary activities. He and his co-workers went underground. "It looks like they are getting ready to shoot us," Lenin said to Trotsky. When the Bolshevik Central Committee met on July 6, Lenin was talked out of giving himself up only after a long debate with Stalin.

Before he again escaped to Finland, this time disguised as a locomotive engineer, Lenin hugged his wife and said, "We may never see each other again." He asked Kamenev to oversee the publication of his draft for a new book, *State and Revolution,* should he be killed. Once in Finland, he found work as a hay maker and had plenty of time to ponder the situation in Russia. More distressing to Lenin than the fact that the street demonstrations had been crushed was his realization that a full-scale anti-Bolshevik campaign was being initiated by the strengthened provisional government and Soviet. The only avenue now open to Lenin was an armed uprising, which he intended to organize and execute before winter arrived.

Kerensky was named prime minister of the provisional government shortly after Lenin's departure, and his control over the government seemed secure for the moment. He moved into what had been the czar's Winter Palace and began to conduct himself more and more like a dictator, but his magnetism as a great speaker was impressing the public far less than it once had. Burning, pillaging, and murder shook the countryside, while factory production in the cities came to a standstill from lack of workers; transportation and law enforcement ceased. Kerensky seemed totally incapable of finding any remedies.

One of Kerensky's few concrete actions as prime minister was to send the czar and his family into exile in Siberia. He should have expelled them from the country immediately following the abdication, but now England revoked its offer to provide asylum, and it was too late to approach other neutral countries like France and Denmark. All this time the royal family, almost completely forgotten by the Russians, had been leading a quiet life under guard at the country estate of Tsarskoye Selo. But Kerensky wanted them as far away from the political arena as possible and also out of harm's way, so he ordered them to a small, remote town in Siberia called Tobolsk. There Nicholas undertook to educate his five children and made sure that the family stayed in good health and exercised. The czar still held out hope that someday he would be restored to power.

Disguised as a worker, Lenin was photographed for an identity card when he left for Finland.

But the only leader in exile who had any realistic chance of attaining power was Lenin. Utterly convinced that a peaceful takeover was no longer possible, he changed his slogan from "All power to the soviets" to "All power to the revolutionary proletariat." The underground Bolshevik organizations in Russia stepped up their recruitment activities despite the fact that several of their leaders had been arrested, and the result was an astounding rise in membership. Lenin masterminded these operations from Finland, with the help of a handful of trusted colleagues like Stalin, who traveled back and forth from the capital with pertinent reading materials and frequent news updates.

Lenin's disguise as a peasant worker was convincing; he looked vastly different wearing a wig, with his beard and moustache shaved off. In the daytime he wrote constantly at a place in the woods he called his "green office"—two tree stumps, one on which he sat and the other on which he leaned to write. A family with seven children called the Emelyanovs watched over Lenin, providing him first with a loft in their barn for sleeping and then with a tent near their lake for receiving visitors. Lenin's main project was to finish *State and Revolution,* a work that, in line with the temper of the times, called for open anarchism as a way of achieving the only true freedom for Russia. "As long as the state exists, there is no freedom, and where there is freedom there will be no state," he wrote. The masses must rise up and destroy all the capitalist vestiges of the bureaucracy and the class system, taking control of the land, the army, and the factories. All citizens would henceforth be equal and would earn equal workers' pay. Only then could the problems of the nation be solved and the people participate in a true Socialist society.

In the letters and articles that he dashed off every day in his Finnish hideaway, Lenin tried to prime his associates for their moment of action. Most of the Bolsheviks were more guarded than Lenin in outlook and tended at first to fear his militancy, but some unexpected events in late August showed everyone just how much latent power the party possessed. One of the top army generals, Lavr Kornilov, decided to use his military strength to topple Kerensky's government and make himself dictator of Russia, restoring some of the conditions of Romanov rule. Kerensky learned of the plan before it could be carried out but was not able to muster enough troops to defend Petrograd against Kornilov's assault. The Soviet was equally powerless, so both organizations were forced to ask the Bolsheviks for assistance. On Lenin's decree, large numbers of Bolsheviks turned out to quash the insurrection, and along the way they gained stores of weapons and invaluable fighting experience. Kerensky was still in charge of the country, but by providing aid, Lenin had craftily made the helplessness of the government's position crystal clear. The army, faithful to the defeated Kornilov, would no longer follow Kerensky's commands. The Bolsheviks had finally begun to feel their strength.

By September the Bolsheviks had won majorities in many local elections, including the Petrograd Soviet, where Trotsky took over as chairman. Domination of the Moscow Soviet and Duma followed. It seemed to many Bolsheviks as if the party could just sit back and collect power through popular demand. But Lenin was as strongly in favor of armed insurrection as ever, because he wanted to permanently sever all ties with the Mensheviks and other Socialist groups, insuring that Bolshevik power would not slip away once it had been attained. He was angered almost to hysteria by the wishy-washy behavior of his colleagues back home and fired off one article after another with the intent of shaming them into action. The Petrograd Bolsheviks wanted to stall until an October 20 meeting of the All-Russian Soviet took place so they could see if the power would come to them through peaceful means. But Lenin argued wildly that the uprising must happen immediately, while the majority of Russians were on their side and before Kerensky could do something drastic to subvert them such as surrender Petrograd to the advancing Germans. In utter frustration, he finally sneaked back across the border into Russia and, by presenting his case directly to the democratically-run Central Committee of the Bolshevik party, Lenin managed to sway the vote on October 10 in favor of the insurrection.

The newspapers got wind of the decision and announced that the uprising would occur on October 20. But some serious dissent within the party developed from an unlikely source—Zinoviev and Kamenev, Lenin's two closest collaborators after Trotsky. At a second vote on the fifteenth, Lenin again won a victory for staging the revolt, but Zinoviev and Kamenev's conviction that it would mean political suicide impelled them to air their dissent in the newspapers. Lenin suggested that the two men be thrown out of the party, but they were merely reprimanded.

It was too late now for a surprise insurrection; everyone already knew what to expect. The only open question was precisely when it would happen. Kerensky stood ready. He knew that his only chance of crushing the Bolsheviks once and for all would be to turn back the revolutionaries whenever they decided to attack. A new warrant was issued for Lenin's arrest. Kerensky alerted loyal troops throughout the country and had the Winter Palace totally surrounded by more than eight hundred soldiers with machine guns and armored cars. But Lenin was exhausted and did nothing for several days. He was hiding out at the apartment of a comrade named Fofanova and sent only a few sporadic messages to the Central Committee.

Independently of Lenin, though, Petrograd came alive with demonstrations on October 22. There was a chance that violence might flare up prematurely, before Lenin was ready to make his move. The Bolsheviks succeeded in convincing the Cossack regiments that they should not march that day, knowing that they were the most volatile of the groups scheduled. In the next two days, the city was like a teakettle, ready to boil. More of Kerensky's troops marched into the city and positioned themselves around the telephone, telegraph, and post offices. Bridges were raised to prevent a flow of traffic and privately-owned cars were requisitioned by the government. The Smolny Institute—the Soviet's headquarters where Trotsky, Zinoviev, and Kamenev were now working—also built up its defenses, and Bolshevik workers tried to win some of Kerensky's garrisons over to their side. Kerensky called a parliamentary meeting to try to rally support for his government against Lenin's imminent attack, but he got only a luke-warm reception. The parliament left Kerensky to stand on his own because he was the one responsible for creating the situation; furthermore, it demanded immediate land grants for peasants and an end to the war. Through all of this activity there had still been no violence anywhere in Petrograd—not yet.

Finally Lenin could not bear to stay in hiding any longer. He feared that his comrades might still call off the uprising, even though a specific time for it had yet to be set. He donned a wig, bandaged his face, and made his way undetected to party headquarters at Smolny Institute. For Fofanova, who feared for his safety, he left a note which read, "I have gone where you did not want me to go." At Smolny, just before dawn, he gave the order to seize control of all the major Petrograd bridges, telephone switchboards, and power stations. The post offices, railroad stations, and most of the public buildings were occupied later. These orders were carried out with no violence, since Kerensky's soldiers did not resist the Bolsheviks. When Kerensky woke up in the Winter Palace on October 25 and saw Bolsheviks teeming on the bridge outside his window, he had cars from the American and British embassies sent over and escaped undercover in the motorcade. He planned to rally troops and return for battle, but only two military groups remained faithful to him—the Junkers (military students) and some women's battalions—and both were stationed in and around the Winter Palace.

Lenin realized that his victory in Petrograd would not be complete until he could take over a few remaining strongholds: the Marinsky Palace where the parliament met, the Petrograd Duma, and, most importantly, the Winter Palace. Nevertheless, he issued a premature proclamation to all the citizens of Russia, declaring that the provisional government had fallen from power, that the Petrograd Soviet was now in authority, and that the true revolutionary causes of democratic peace, land ownership, and industrial control were now in the hands of the people. Then he sternly lectured the Bolshevik Institute officers at Smolny, ordering them to wrap up the coup immediately.

Soon the Winter Palace was the last holdout. Its seizure by the Bolsheviks took a whole day. Bolsheviks infiltrated the building in small groups, allowing themselves to be disarmed without a fight, and then tried to harangue the Junkers and the women's battalions into joining them. Eventually, the defenders of the fortress could not handle the enormous Bolshevik crowds. When the battleship Aurora finally fired some blank shells at the palace from the Neva River around 2:00 A.M., a large group of armed revolutionaries took that as their signal to storm in and seize the building.

At 4:00 A.M. on October 26, Lenin was at last assured that Petrograd was entirely his. Too tired for celebration, he drove to a friend's apartment to sleep for a few hours. That evening, he appeared before the assembled congress of Soviets, still haggard but exhilarated. First he presented his peace decree to the hall crowded with workers, soldiers, and peasants. It was a call for immediate peace among all the nations involved in World War I and for a three-month armistice with Germany. It was intended as a first step toward world socialism. Lenin spoke simply and efficiently, as always, and when he was finished, his audience cheered and wept, threw their hats in the air, and sang the "International." Lenin's deep, melodic voice could be heard above all the others.

His other decree of the evening had to do with land. Private property would no longer exist, because all land would belong to the state. The decree was designed to immediately swing all the peasants in the countryside over to Bolshevism, and Lenin made no bones about the fact that he had borrowed the specifics from the Social Revolutionary platform. The members of the congress were baffled, but approved the decree. And so, of Lenin's three "campaign" promises—peace, land, and bread—he had acted on two on his very first day of power. Unfortunately, the third was not only the most difficult to attain, but it would haunt him throughout the first few years of his administration.

One final piece of business was taken care of that night: the new government executives were named. The title of "ministers" did not seem appropriate because it was reminiscent of czarist times, so Trotsky invented the term "People's Commissars." Lenin, naturally, became the head, and key Bolsheviks were assigned posts on the ruling body, or commissariat. Trotsky became commissar of foreign affairs and Stalin, commissar of nationalities. Since most Bolsheviks had no previous experience in administration, their new jobs were often confusing and even frightening to them. They argued a lot among themselves, and, because they were affected for a while by the ongoing government workers' strike, not much was accomplished in their first days in office.

Hardly any one truly believed that Lenin's regime would stay in power for more than a few hours or a few days. But then Moscow was taken and other major cities joined in support of the Bolsheviks. Kerensky, the major threat to Lenin's victory, was unable to muster a large enough force to invade Petrograd. He did return with a few hundred Cossacks, but Lenin sent a larger army to counter them, led by army officers who by now preferred to see almost anyone except Kerensky in power. The two forces argued when they met, but no blood was shed. Kerensky, fearing that he would be thrown on the mercy of the Bolsheviks, escaped, dressed as a sailor. He eventually made his way to America and died in New York in 1970 at the age of eighty.

With Kerensky out of the picture for good, it became apparent that Lenin was the undisputed leader of Russia, and his main goal was to build the new Socialist order. No task, however, could have proved more difficult. He inherited a nation torn apart by a seemingly eternal war, suffering, starvation, and anarchy. He was still much despised by many within his own country, not to mention abroad. He was no statesman; he was, by his own admission, merely a revolutinary, a terrorist, with a very strong intuitive sense. The country would now see if this man from Simbirsk could make good on all his tall promises, substantiate all his bold theories. The people were in such dire straits that they wanted results—fast.

The nation at first seemed almost unmanageable. Some

feeble counterrevolts were crushed immediately by Lenin's forces. But there was a strong Cossack contingent in Moscow prepared to fight the Bolsheviks. The railway union, fearing that a civil war might break out, refused to transport Lenin's troops out of Petrograd or anti-Bolshevik troops into Petrograd. Lenin had all publishing houses and newspapers not under Bolshevik control cease their operations and created a central censorship board. His tactics were revolting even to many members of his own party, who feared that such dictatorial measures would result in a bloodbath if they failed and in a regime not unlike the czar's if they succeeded.

Lenin, however, was prepared to hold onto power by whatever means necessary. He felt bound by his word to hold an election for the Constituent Assembly, the democratic parliament that was to have been formed long ago by the incompetent provisional government. This organization, which would serve to draft a constitution, had been the dream of all the liberal and revolutionary factions in Russia for the past hundred years. Lenin knew that his Bolshevik party, with its twenty-five thousand members, might not yet be strong enough to win such a popular election. Yet the balloting took place from November 25 to 27 in 1917, and to this day it remains the only free election that Russia ever had. As projected, the Bolsheviks suffered a major defeat to the Social Revolutionary party. If Lenin had acquiesced in the outcome of the election, the Constituent Assembly would have seated 707 Social Revolutionaries and only 175 Bolsheviks, and would undoubtedly have tried to undo Lenin's newfound authority. Like the czar with his troublesome Duma, Lenin simply had the Constituent Assembly dissolved. Henceforth Russia would be a one-party state.

Lenin realized that a campaign of terror was the only way he could secure his political gains. On his orders large numbers of known political enemies were imprisoned and a special organization called the Cheka (Extraordinary Commission to Combat Counter-Revolution and Sabotage) was created to subvert all opponents to Bolshevism. The Cheka was nothing more than a secret police force as ruthless as its counterpart under the czar. Hostages were held in the prisons of most major cities, to be executed if any Bolshevik leaders should be assassinated. Troops invaded the countryside, seizing food from the peasants to replenish the starving cities.

Lenin's peace decree had not had much clout with the other warring nations, all of them capitalist societies that despite their conflicts were uniformly opposed to what they considered the "Red threat" in Russia. (The color red had become the symbol of Communism: following the revolution, the Bolsheviks had adopted a red flag as their emblem, inspired by the red flag of insurrection in the French Revolution.) Lenin knew that the war had to be ended at once, before the Germans could invade Russia. Other threats loomed as well: the Ukrainians were rising up with increasing strength to achieve their independence, and the Cossacks and other military forces in the south promised to pose a serious counterrevolutionary challenge. Troops from the United States, France, and England entered Russia to help turn back the Germans, but they also aided "White" or anti-Bolshevik armies in battling the revolutionary regime in Russia. In desperation Lenin finally accepted Germany's proposed peace terms and signed the Treaty of Brest-Litovsk in March 1918. The conditions of the document were humiliating. He gave up one-fourth of Russia's territory, including Poland, the Ukraine, the Baltic states, a large chunk of Byelorussia, and some land along the Turkish border. Accordingly Russia lost one-third of its population, as well as sizable farming regions and most of its industrialized areas. Lenin planned to honor the agreement only partially and counted on the treaty buying him some time to set his country on a productive, orderly path again. Besides, he still hoped for an international Socialist revolution; and, if it actually happened, the German monarchy would be one of the first European regimes to fall.

As soon as the treaty was signed, Lenin moved the Russian capital from Petrograd to Moscow because Petrograd was so exposed to possible German and even White Army attack. The decision was not a popular one, for the Petrograd workers felt that they were being abandoned to the Germans. Lenin and his co-workers had to escape by train to Moscow under cover of darkness. Once there they settled down to live and work in the run-down buildings of the Kremlin, a walled-in complex from which the czars had ruled centuries before. Lenin and Trotsky conferred as they passed each other in the hallways several times a day. Lenin and Krupskaya inhabited a modest five-room apartment on the first floor of the Kovalevsky building, which was sparsely decorated so as not to suggest any of the former affluence of the czar.

In the spring and summer of 1918, conspiracies mounted against the Bolsheviks. Czech forces engineered uprisings and takeovers in Siberian cities and on the Trans-Siberian Railroad. The Allied nations, still fighting their war against Germany, readied an invasion to get Russia back on their side. The Social Revolutionaries initiated a wave of assassinations of Bolsheviks and visiting German diplomats, even seizing the Cheka's headquarters in the new capital. Lenin managed to put down the Social Revolutionary rebellion, but the open revolt was replaced by an equally serious climate of fear and loathing of the new government. Trotsky traveled tirelessly by train through the country, trying to rally a Red Army along the way from former czarist soldiers and Bolshevik city workers. As persuasive as ever, he was able to conjure up a limited but strong base of support.

While all of this was happening, the czar and his family met with a tragic fate. They had been moved from their backward Siberian town of Tobolsk in May 1918 because Lenin feared that a White Guard plot to rescue them might stand a chance of succeeding in such an out-of-the-way place. They were sent to Ekaterinburg, a Bolshevik stronghold in the Urals (it was rumored that Lenin himself planned to take refuge in Ekaterinburg if both Moscow and Petrograd became endangered). There they were confined to a large house, watched constantly by Red Guards, and allowed no communication with the outside world. Nicholas II seemed to sense what was coming because he stopped writing in his diary with his usual regularity. Lenin was unsure at first how to handle the situation. He could either stage a trial and then have the family executed, as everyone seemed to anticipate, or he could simply have them killed. Finally, he chose the latter course. The czar, his wife, and his five children were all led into one room of their house and shot to death. Their corpses were stripped completely, transported to a mine a few miles away, and destroyed with fire and acid until only a few small pieces of their bones remained. Elsewhere, in the city of Perm, the Grand Duke Mikhail, who had abdicated to the provisional government after his brother Nicholas had stepped down from power in 1917, was murdered by the Bolshevik Cheka. So was the czar's close friend in Tobolsk, Archbishop Germogen. On July 17, the news was released from the capital that only the czar had been executed and that the rest of the royal family was safe. Incredibly, the government's reticence kept the truth about the massacre from being discovered for several years. Because of Lenin's initial secrecy and the lack of Romanov remains, legends persist to this day that one or more of the family members may have survived and escaped to the West.

As Lenin continued to pit his loyal Reds against the counterrevolutionary Whites in what was fast becoming a full-blown civil war, the country fell deeper into anarchy and despair. From 1918 to 1920, an estimated seven million Russians died of starvation because of the pitiful pace of both agricultural and industrial production. (Agricultural output was reduced by half between 1917 and 1921 and in 1917 industrial production dropped to one third of its level in 1913. By 1920 it was less than 13 percent of production in 1913.) The simple people were terrorized in the cities and the countryside by bands of robbers, deserters, former prisoners of war, and foreign adventurers. Cannibalism was reported in some of the backwoods areas. Lenin knew that he had to stop the civil war before he could do anything to help the common people. "War Communism" became the name of his new policy, where any tactics—including open and widespread terror— were permissible to preserve and maintain the revolutionary regime.

In August 1918 the head of the Petrograd Cheka was assassinated and Lenin himself was seriously injured by two bullets from the gun of an ardent Social Revolutionary named Fanya Kaplan. In retaliation more than one thousand hostages in Petrograd, the Kronstadt fortress, Perm, Moscow, and other locations were executed. Long lists of their names filled the newspapers. But by the time Lenin had recovered from the assassination attempt that fall, the threat to his power was just as acute. The Czechs and the Whites, having secured Siberia, advanced toward Moscow. Trotsky took his Red Army to a small Volga town called Sviazhsk and prepared to do battle. Despite widespread desertions, after a bloody battle the fearless Trotsky and his five hundred loyal men were victorious. All through 1919, alternative governments in cities and towns along the Volga fell one by one to the Bolsheviks. Trotsky slowly collected triumphs and the backing of the peasants, who came to realize that the brutish Whites would be no more desirable as leaders than the Reds. By 1920 the civil war subsided.

When Lenin took over the leadership of Russia, he had decided on two yardsticks by which to measure the success of his regime. The first was peasant support, which he now seemed to be getting. The second was the advent of world revolution. When World War I finally came to a close at the end of 1918, Germany was the loser and its people revolted from within. For a while, with the naval fleet staging mutinies and soviets springing up in the cities, it appeared that the German Socialists would follow the Bolshevik lead. Lenin watched the events closely and joyfully, only to have his hopes dashed. The Social Democratic party—more conservative than Lenin's counterpart, the Spartacus League—was voted into power and its leaders had key figures of the opposition killed, including Karl Liebknecht and Rosa Luxemburg. With them died Lenin's dream of an international proletarian revolution.

Through all these crises, Lenin never stopped comparing actual events with his idealistic theories that had been formed in the prerevolutionary years. He realized that after all those years of waging an underground war in the name of Socialism, he had succeeded in establishing nothing less than a ruthless dictatorship. The revolution would have to happen in two stages, he reasoned. First would come the War Communism that would end all military strife at home and abroad and get Russia back on its feet socially and economically. Then the Socialist stage would be introduced, where the state and all social classes would be abolished. Thus far, the world war and the civil war had been terminated. But the anarchy that the Bolsheviks themselves had helped to spawn before the revolution still reigned across the land. At a March 1920 meeting of the Moscow Soviet, Lenin argued that the time had not yet come for the state to dissolve itself. "To object to the necessity of a central power, a dictatorship . . . has become impossible after the experience we have gone through," he announced. It was a clash between theory and practice. Once again the theory would have to wait just a while longer to become reality.

In the winter of 1921 anti-Bolshevik insurrections started up again. The cities had been cut off from food for months, bread rations were almost nonexistent, and, despite inflation, the pay for work was a fraction of what it had been before the war. The Petrograd population had shrunk from 2,500,000 in 1914 to 500,000 in 1921, but now those people who remained revolted with strikes and demonstrations. All the shops were closed down, roadblocks encircled the city, and armies worked their way through the streets in an attempt to impose curfews. Zinoviev, then the leading Bolshevik official in Petrograd, cabled Moscow for military backup. Mensheviks and Social Revolutionaries who had somehow escaped detection by the Cheka, appeared on the streets with pamphlets and demands. Finally the sailors from two battleships moored in the icy harbor arrived in town with revolutionary demands of their own: freedom of agitation, speech, and assembly; new elections to the Soviet by secret ballot; freedom for all political prisoners and investigations into the charges against all those jailed and in concentration camps; better rations; removal of roadblocks; and so on. Essentially

V. I. Lenin, head of the Bolshevik government, addresses a crowd of Red Army troops in Moscow's Sverdlov Square in 1920.

the large number of sailors wanted what most of the revolutionaries, including Lenin, had fought for exactly four years before when they had risen up against the czar: an end to dictatorship, and power in the hands of the people ("All power to the soviets").

Lenin, of course, would not comply. Ironically he was put in the position of battling the very forces whose brave support had made his accession to power possible in the first place. Zinoviev called for the immediate surrender of the Kronstadt sailors. Trotsky arrived in Petrograd and repeated the demand for surrender, threatening that otherwise he would "shoot [the rebels] like pheasants." That is exactly what happened. On March 7, Trotsky's army attacked the Kronstadt fortress, where the sailors had stationed themselves, and after eleven bloody days of assault and counterassault, more than ten thousand Reds and sailors were dead, wounded, or missing. Only around six hundred Kronstadt supporters had been killed, whereas a thousand were hurt and eight thousand escaped to Finland. The Red Army casualties were much worse, but Trotsky was victorious nonetheless. As a result of the Kronstadt Rebellion, as it was called, Petrograd was left a ghostly shell of a city and Lenin was the undisputed leader of Russia. Although a good portion of the population still seethed with hatred for his regime, opposition to the Bolsheviks now became extinct.

On the heels of the uprising, in mid-March, Lenin introduced his New Economic Policy (NEP) to the Tenth Party Congress. With it, he hoped to achieve several economic goals: an end to the exodus from the cities, a curtailing of the rampant inflation, a rise in industrial production, and, most importantly, a better relationship with the peasants. The NEP introduced free enterprise to Russia. No longer would food be seized from the peasants for government distribution according to the mandates of War Communism. Instead a tax would be placed on food, and peasants would be free to sell their products in the marketplace. The NEP promised to save Russia by breaking down the barriers between city and country, by restoring a steady flow of food to the cities, and by establishing economic order through private businesses and foreign trade. But it smacked of capitalism, which Lenin loathed. The policy was just one more compromise that Lenin had to make, taking him further from his ideals in order to preserve hope for the eventual realization of his faraway Socialist dream.

Apart from the institutionalization of the New Economic Policy, Lenin did not put any of the power back into the hands of the people. The ruthless way that the Bolsheviks had handled the Kronstadt Rebellion was the last straw for countless artists, writers, musicians, and citizens at large, who completely relinquished their hopes for a democratic, constitutional society in Russia and went abroad to live as expatriates. Maxim Gorky, the writer, was also disillusioned and decided to leave. He would not return to Russia for ten years, but before he departed, he helped to save millions of lives in his homeland by putting out a worldwide plea for food and medicine. America responded immediately; Herbert Hoover, then head of the American Relief administration, sent eight hundred thousand tons of food, which was distributed in the cities and sent by train deep into the countryside. Russia was on its feet again.

The endless matters, both small and large, of making his administration more efficient and improving the economic conditions of Russia occupied Lenin's time. From his Kremlin office, he composed scores of memoranda on practical approaches to appeasing the workers, spreading electricity to the distant regions, handling money matters, and even on the necessity of keeping Kremlin elevators in good repair. When he became ill while on vacation in August 1921, Lenin assumed that he was just overworked to the point of exhaustion after four years of nonstop political activity.

All this time, Russia had not established diplomatic relations or trade with the major European nations and the United States, and such ties would not begin to come about until 1924. The delay can be attributed primarily to two factors. First, countries abroad were hesitant to establish trade or extend credit when the new government had yet to settle its massive war debts and inherited czarist debts. And second, in the first years of its existence, the Bolsheviks persistently interfered in the internal political affairs of foreign countries by means of an organization known as the Comintern (the Third or Communist International). Lenin had not given up his dream of world revolution, and the Comintern, founded by him in 1919, was a representation of the Communist parties he helped to spawn in various countries for the purpose of engineering violent overthrows of their governments and institutions. Although the Comintern was a democratically-run body, in which each Communist party had an equal vote, the political powers outside of Russia rightly perceived it as a Russian invention and instrument, and they kept their diplomatic distance from the new nation for several years.

While living abroad before the Russian revolution, Lenin had done all the work for the Bolshevik party, organizing everything himself. But now, as the leader of the government, he had to delegate responsibility, and his four top men handled many of his important affairs: Stalin managed the party administration, Trotsky presided over the army, Zinoviev ruled Petrograd, and Kamenev ruled Moscow. Trotsky had never been completely accepted by the other leading Bolsheviks, who treated him with distrust because he had jumped on their political bandwagon so late in the revolutionary struggle. Zinoviev, Kamenev, and Stalin, however, had a strong comraderie among them because they had set up the Bolshevik apparatus and operations in Russia while Lenin was still trapped in exile in Switzerland. All three were much less radical in viewpoint than Lenin, and over the years their differences became increasingly apparent. Only Stalin quarrelled openly with Lenin, perhaps because Lenin was so fixed on making the party machinery run more smoothly, which was Stalin's domain. Stalin was a surly, unlikable man who at first supported Lenin on all the major issues, but then poked fun at him behind his back. Lenin blamed Stalin for setting up a "bureaucratic swamp" and early in 1922 appointed two new Bolsheviks to devise a more efficient system. If they had completed their task, Stalin would probably have been unseated in the process.

But then Lenin got sick again, this time from migraines and insomnia. Forced by his doctors to rest for extended periods of time and to miss countless meetings and consultations, he felt compelled to shift most of his administrative responsibilities, and he offered Stalin the prestigious position of general party secretary. At the same time Lenin asked Trotsky to become his personal first deputy, but Trotsky refused. While still in bed, Lenin created a new criminal code which justified and legalized the use of terror by the state so as to preserve order. Unwittingly he had undone himself and set his country up for disaster; he had elevated Stalin to a position of high responsibility and then passed a law that Stalin would later use ruthlessly to implement his own selfish plans.

On May 26, 1922, Lenin suffered a minor stroke that left him with impaired speech and partial paralysis on his right side. Inactive throughout the summer, he could only watch as Stalin consolidated strength and grew more cocky and sure of himself. Then, in the fall, when Lenin was well enough to resume his work full-time, they locked horns publicly over the drafting of a new constitution. Stalin had come from the small southern republic of Georgia, which had been annexed to Russia, yet he espoused a chauvinistic plan whereby all the small Soviet nationalities would be put in a subordinate position to Russia proper. Lenin, on the other hand, advocated the formation of a federation of republics. Stalin was openly rude to Lenin in the meeting room, and both men separately expressed to colleagues in private their determination to win their respective goals. The debate was delayed because Lenin came down with a toothache. And then, on December 13, Lenin had a second mild stroke after arguing with Stalin and one of his supporters on the nationalities question. (The Union of Soviet Socialist Republics, or USSR, was officially organized on December 30, and consisted originally of only three large republics. In 1924 it was reorganized on a nationalities basis, and its republics, which now totaled fifteen, were added gradually over the next twelve years.)

Lenin knew that he might die soon or become completely incapacitated, so he sought to undermine Stalin as quickly

and completely as possible. Lenin dictated articles and letters from his bed, including a plan (that was never implemented) for enlarging the party's governing Central Committee and reducing the functions of the central government. Thus, Stalin would have been demoted. Lenin also spent as much time with Trotsky as he could, training him to carry out the Leninist political platform. Stalin suspected what was going on and phoned Krupskaya to harangue her for letting her husband conduct business when he had been ordered to rest. He threatened to have her arrested. Krupskaya told Lenin what had happened and in March, after an inexplicable delay of three months, Lenin demanded an apology from Stalin and got one.

Yet another stroke on March 9, 1923, left Lenin completely unable to speak or to move. He recovered enough by winter to walk and to read a bit. But then, on January 21, 1924, he died suddenly. He carried to his grave the realization that his revolution had veered out of his control, onto a new course that his rival would chart. Russia would never pass through the prerequisite phase of dictatorship to reach Lenin's second stage of true Socialism, a classless society free of bureaucracy and internal strife. Lenin's revolutionary vision would never become a reality.

Lenin, with his wife Krupskaya, convalesces from a stroke in 1922 at his home in Gorky, near Moscow.

AFTERWORD

Word of Lenin's death spread like wildfire from the snow-covered town of Gorky to the rest of the world. The immediate reaction within Russia was one of profound grief and suffering. This was partly due to the shock effect that the news had; until the very end, all of the papers and official health bulletins had been highly optimistic that Lenin would recover. Perhaps the authorities had kept up the false hopes because they realized what a symbol of strength Lenin had become.

Despite all of the negative aspects of Lenin's years in power, the Russians had publicly and uniformly admired their leader since the time that he had been shot in the unsuccessful assassination attempt of 1918. Lenin's politics and personal life—his speeches, his modest life-style and low salary, his intellect, and his willingness to listen to and heed the simple people—had been scrutinized and lauded in the press. He had been for them a sort of father figure, whose genius had guided the country out of its seemingly insurmountable tangle of crises.

Now, suddenly, he was gone. The loss seemed to affect each and every Russian on a personal level. The people felt abandoned, as if they had been left on their own to cope with a situation that they were not equipped to handle. The public outpouring of bereavement was overwhelming, and threatened to reach the proportions of mass hysteria. Administrative leaders, particularly Stalin, realized that the most effective way of avoiding a national crisis would be to channel the grief into a fresh surge of patriotism. This they accomplished by immortalizing their leader.

Lenin's body was transported by train to Moscow. Along every foot of the thirty-mile route, Russians waited silently in the bitter cold for the passing of the funeral car. More than half a million people made a pilgrimage to pay their respects at Moscow's Hall of Columns where the body lay in state. And then, on Stalin's order and against Lenin's previously specified wishes, Petrograd was renamed Leningrad and Lenin was neither buried nor cremated, but embalmed. A wooden building just outside the Kremlin wall in Moscow's Red Square was constructed in three short days, and the body was placed inside for all to view. Sixteen months later, a permanent structure—a red granite mausoleum—was built on the spot. Russia never had to acknowledge fully the loss of its leader because he was still visible among them, still as accessible as before. And Lenin, who lies to this day with a faint smile on his lips and who seems to be merely sleeping in his glass box, has become a sacred national object.

Theodore Dreiser, the American author, wrote in 1928 that "so long as he is there, so long as he does not change, Communism is safe and the new Russia will prosper." Whether one adheres to this superstition or not, Communism has indeed remained safe and has prospered since 1924; however, for this, Russia has paid a staggering price. The dying Lenin's worst fear came true. Stalin jockeyed himself into power by playing the other key party members against each other and gradually eliminating his opposition. First, he enlisted the aid of Zinoviev and Kamenev to drive Trotsky out of the party. Within four years, he had engineered Trotsky's exile to a small town called Alma Ata near the Chinese border. In 1929 Trotsky was forced out of the country altogether, going first to Turkey, then to Norway, and finally settling in Mexico where he was assassinated by one of Stalin's henchmen in 1940. Stalin also split the powerful duo of Zinoviev and Kamenev.

Once at the helm of the government, he displayed the full magnitude of his lust for absolute power and his acute personal paranoia. During his twenty-five years in office, millions were liquidated without benefit of trial in the waves of purges and executions that he initiated to cleanse the party of its "enemies." Hundreds of thousands more languished in the network of labor camps that he set up. The progress of the arts and sciences came to a halt because Stalin fancied himself a genius who had to have the last word on all matters of culture and state. Imagining threats to his power coming from all corners of society, he safeguarded his rule by presiding over one of the most ruthless dictatorial regimes in history.

In the more moderate administrations of Nikita Krushchev and Leonid Brezhnev that followed Stalin's death in 1953, the full horrors of Stalin's reign of terror have been revealed. Stalin has become a national villain, and his name is now barely whispered in the very land that he once ruled with such a vicelike grip.

And so, more than half a century after his death, Lenin has maintained his place as the greatest popular hero of the Russians. He represents for them the very pillar of their modern society, the core of their Communist ideology. During his lifetime, Lenin accomplished the impossible: he assumed leadership of a huge country that had been under autocratic rule for more than three hundred years; he maintained his power in the face of world war, counterrevolution, and civil war; he stabilized the nation's battered economy; and he created a new ideal of society based on the writings of Karl Marx and on his own vision for Russia. Lenin also had his share of failures. The campaigns of terror that protected his power through one national crisis after another were woefully reminiscent of those aspects of czarist rule that had sparked the revolution in the first place. And his inability to put the power swiftly into the hands of the people, as he had promised, led to tragedy on a grand scale, because his premature death was followed by the unstoppable ascent of the tyrannical Stalin.

Lenin was no god. He was a mere mortal who, through a combination of chance and calculation, founded one of the two reigning superpowers in the world today. Every day that he has slept in his resting place in Red Square, his enormous impact has been felt, not just in his own country but also throughout the world. And although he will never wake, neither is it likely that he will soon be allowed to die.

FOR FURTHER READING

Ascher, Abraham. *The Kremlin: Russia From Tsar to Commissar.* New York: Newsweek Book Division, 1972.

Chamberlin, William Henry. *The Russian Revolution, 1917–1921.* New York: Grosset and Dunlap, 1973.

Conquest, Robert. *Lenin* (Modern Masters Series). London: Fontana-Collins, 1972.

Hughes, H. Stuart. *Contemporary Europe: A History,* Third Edition. Englewood Cliffs, New Jersey: Prentice-Hall, 1971.

Krupskaya, N.K. *Memories of Lenin.* New York: International Publishers, 1930.

Lenin, V.I. *What Is to Be Done? Burning Questions of Our Movement.* Peking: Foreign Languages Press, 1978.

_____. *State and Revolution.* New York: International Publishers, 1971.

McNeal, Robert H. *Bride of the Revolution: Krupskaya and Lenin.* Ann Arbor: The University of Michigan Press, 1972.

Pasternak, Boris. *Doctor Zhivago.* New York: Pantheon Books, 1958.

Rabinowitch, Alexander. *The Bolsheviks Come to Power: The Revolution of 1917 in Petrograd.* New York: W.W. Norton and Company, 1976.

Reed, John. *Ten Days That Shook the World.* New York: New American Library, 1967.

Salisbury, Harrison E. *Black Night, White Snow: Russia's Revolutions, 1905–1917.* New York: Da Capo, 1981.

_____. *Russia in Revolution, 1900–1930.* New York: Holt, Rinehart & Winston, 1978.

Shub, David. *Lenin.* Garden City, New York: Doubleday & Company, 1948.

Silverman, Saul N., ed. *Lenin* (Great Lives Observed Series). Englewood Cliffs, New Jersey: Prentice-Hall, 1972.

Solzhenitsyn, Alexander. *Lenin in Zurich.* New York: Penguin, 1980.

Theen, Rolf H.W. *Lenin: Genesis and Development of a Revolutionary.* Princeton, New Jersey: Princeton University Press, 1973.

Trotsky, Leon. *Lenin: Notes for a Biographer.* New York: G.P. Putnam's Sons, 1971.

_____ *1905.* New York: Vintage, 1971.

_____ *The Russian Revolution.* Garden City, New York: Doubleday & Company, 1959.

Tucker, Robert C., ed. *The Lenin Anthology.* New York: W.W. Norton and Company, 1975.

Ulam, Adam B. *The Bolsheviks: The Intellectual, Personal, and Political History of the Triumph of Communism in Russia.* New York: Collier Books, 1965.

Valentinov, Nikolay. *Encounters With Lenin.* New York: Oxford University Press, 1968.

Wilson, Edmund. *To the Finland Station.* New York: Farrar, Straus, and Giroux, 1972.

Wolfe, Bertram D. *Three Who Made a Revolution.* New York: Dell Publishing Company, 1964.

INDEX